FPL ELITE:

HOW TO BE THE BEST AT FANTASY PREMIER LEAGUE

MATT WHELAN

First Edition

Cover design by: OGLY Diseño Online

ISBN (paperback): 978-1-7398608-6-8

ISBN (ebook): 978-1-7398608-7-5

ISBN (hardcover): 978-1-7398608-8-2

Published by Arrowcroft Press

ARROWCROFT
PRESS

For Rachael

The list of things I must thank you for is endless,
yet growing every day

CONTENTS

INTRODUCTION

In February 2022 – just days after Vladimir Putin had rocked the world by ordering the invasion of Ukraine – I found myself standing, wrapped in a towel, on the living room floor of our holiday villa in the Caribbean, anxiously watching the television screen.

We had waited for this family holiday for three years. The original booking, made in 2019, for the summer of 2020, was cancelled due to Covid restrictions. The ban on flights was lifted in time for the postponed holiday – rebooked for the summer of 2021 – but this time my wife caught Covid less than a week before we were due to fly, so once again the holiday was postponed, this time to February 2022. But it wasn't just international travel which Covid was playing hell with. The Premier League schedule was also a complete mess. Fans of Premier League football had never before experienced such disruption and this, of course, had a massive impact on Fantasy Premier League (FPL), with blank and double Gameweeks all over the place.

My wife and kids were in the pool, enjoying the tropical sunshine. I had made an excuse to go back to the villa so that I could turn on the TV and catch up on what was happening. But it was not the world-changing, World War III-ushering, Armageddon-threatening news in Eastern Europe I was so nervously watching. Liverpool were playing Leeds in the second instalment of their double Gameweek, and I was one of the very few managers who hadn't played the Triple Captain chip on Mohamed Salah.

I had got off relatively lightly during the first instalment of the double Gameweek. Salah had scored a single goal against Norwich but (annoyingly) had bagged all three bonus points. Ten points with a game left to play. It could have been worse, but a lot depended on how he did against Leeds. I was about to find out.

It's a thoroughly confusing and unpleasant feeling watching a player you own in FPL, who also plays for the team you support, and yet praying they don't score or get an assist. But many engaged FPL managers will be all too familiar with this contradictory sensation. Sadly, my prayers went unanswered as Salah went on to score twice and get an assist. Devastating! The only small crumb of solace I could take from the game was that Sadio Mané went on to score a brace, which was enough to just nick a bonus point from Salah right at the death – Ha! In your face Triple Captainers! – but the damage was done. Twenty-eight points. Eightyfriggin'-four points if you played the Triple Captain on him, which, of course, almost everyone had.

Whether you're new to FPL, or remember this famous Gameweek well, you will probably be wondering why I didn't play the Triple Captain chip on FPL's most consistently explosive player, in a Gameweek in which he was facing both Norwich and Leeds. I'd like to say that it was because I had already used it, but the truth of the matter is, I had decided to play my Free Hit that week instead and was therefore prohibited from using the Triple Captain.

The timing of this – now twice rescheduled – holiday was absolutely awful in relation to FPL. Deadlines were coming in thick and fast during a ten-day period in which I had decided to play both my Free Hit and second Wildcard (the two chips which require the most intensive planning), in amongst double and blank Gameweeks. Fortunately, it was a chill out (rather than an exploration) holiday, so while my wife was reading, I was sitting with my laptop, pen and paper, planning my moves.

I had given the Triple Captain scenario a lot of thought but had decided to play my Free Hit in double Gameweek 26. Due to Covid postponements, the 2021/22 season was the first – and so far, only – time that we have been given a second Free Hit – a generous gift from our overlords in FPL Towers. Many managers were planning to use this second

Free Hit to navigate blank Gameweek 27, which my team was well set up for. Sadly, my team looked like a pile of sheep's droppings for double Gameweek 26, one in which there were many teams playing twice.

My logic was that if I used my Free Hit here, I would instantly gain an advantage over those who were going to use hits to optimise their team. Additionally, I could really attack the Gameweek by fielding 11 x doublers, I'd be able to navigate Gameweek 27 without making any transfers, and finally, I would still have my Triple Captain chip to play later on in the season. The only downside, it seemed, was opting against Mo Salah in two easy fixtures. A large downside indeed.

As things turned out, playing the Free Hit was (remarkably!) the better option, but only slightly. With double-digit hauls from Virgil van Dijk, Wilfried Zaha, Wout Weghorst (remember him?) and Alexandre Lacazette, I finished the Gameweek on a whopping 150 points! And, of course, still had my Triple Captain chip up my sleeve.

For those of you who read my previous book *FPL Obsessed: Tips for Success in Fantasy Premier League*, you will know that I haven't had much joy with the Triple Captain chip, and the same was true this season. I decided to play it three Gameweeks later, in double Gameweek 29, when Liverpool played Brighton and Arsenal. Sadly, Salah –

renowned for his guaranteed game time and injury-free career – only managed 90 minutes between both fixtures and scored 10 points (compared to the 28 points from Gameweek 26).

Despite the above, I ended up with a season finish of 68k. A decrease from the previous season (23k), but a respectable finish nevertheless.

As the season drew to a close, I came into contact with a lovely chap called Tom who contacted me on behalf of Fantasy Football Fix (more on that later). If you are an engaged member of the FPL community, or an avid FPL manager, then there's a good chance you are already familiar with Fix. If you don't know who they are, they are one of the top websites dedicated to FPL tools and statistics, their direct rivals being Fantasy Football Scout and Fantasy Football Hub. They were also amongst the first to innovate in the area of AI-based prediction models.

They are now home to the 'Elite XI' concept; a group of the world's finest – objectively speaking – FPL managers. I was[1] lucky enough to work with this elite group of managers and gain unfettered access to their insight, strategy and mindset.

---

[1] And, at the time of writing, still am.

This book is a distilled product of all the information I have gathered from spending years working closely with the world's very best FPL managers.

If you are interested in discovering the secrets of the FPL elite, then read on.

PART ONE

FIX AND THE ELITE XI

FANTASY FOOTBALL FIX

Have you ever found yourself chatting to a stranger about Premier League football and wondered, nervously, if you should try to shift the conversation to FPL? Well, that's precisely what happened in the spring of 2015, during a chance encounter between two strangers in a gym.

Sam, a less-than-dedicated gym user (to put it politely), met Adam amidst the equipment. A safe conversation about football quickly evolved to Sam asking, "So, do you play FPL?"

Typically, the answer to this question is either "No, but I've heard of it" or "Yes, I do." When the latter answer is given, then it is usually someone who plays on a casual basis, perhaps in a work mini-league, or against close friends. On more scarce occasions, you may bump into someone who is FPL obsessed, or a member of the online FPL community.

What Sam wasn't expecting was that the stranger in crutches he had just met was, in fact, developing an algorithm designed to help him consistently achieve Top 10k finishes. "Yes, I play FPL" is something of an understatement in this case.

Adam's original intention was to keep this algorithm to himself. But Sam had other ideas. The concept of bringing artificial intelligence (AI) to the FPL community was spinning madly around his brain.

While neither of these gentlemen could have known at the time, the very first foundation of Fantasy Football Fix – colloquially known as just 'Fix' – had been laid.

2016

Fast forward a year and the beta version of the website was launched. The concept of Fix was simple: provide a clean and user-friendly platform which would allow users to apply Adam's unique algorithm to refine their own FPL squad. As the year progressed, new ideas were implemented. Concepts such as 'live rank' – now regarded as essential by most engaged FPL managers – were coming to the forefront of their thinking. By the end of 2016, Fix had over 20 unique FPL tools.

2017

It wasn't until the year after that the company started gaining real traction. Always looking to move forward, they partnered with Opta. The concept of Expected Goals (xG) prior to 2017 had been the domain of the football analytics community, a majorly underappreciated subcommunity at the time, and a bunch of people often (and unfairly) regarded as nothing more than geeks who had never kicked a ball in their lives.

The day before the 2017/18 season kicked off, the BBC announced that the British footballing institution, *Match of the Day*, would be featuring xG as part of their coverage. This was a major win for the analytics community and would pave the way for the unstoppable rise of sports data and its myriad of practical applications.

Fix went one step beyond using Opta's data for xG. They developed their own version. Using Opta F24 live feeds, they were able to import player co-ordinates in real time. This was a game changer for the Gameweek Live tool. Now FPL managers could see every kick of a ball in real time and view player heatmaps live.

2018

What had once been an academic project was now a serious website with a growing user base. Fix needed to invest heavily in getting a server which could cope with increasing demand, and scale with the forecast future growth of the business. New tools were being added all the time, including Fix Rivals, a tool which allows managers to keep detailed tabs on their biggest mini-league adversaries.

2019

A year on and Fix was going strong, with a growing war chest of tools and features. In 2019, the data science team was expanded and members were tasked with creating new statistics which could help FPL managers. One particular problem was the mystery of why, in some Gameweeks, FPL managers were achieving incredible scores, yet still falling down the overall ranks (or vice versa). Because FPL success/failure is determined by your performance relative to those around you, a solution was needed to find a way of narrowing down player ownership around a specific rank tier. Moreover, the system needed to allow for the fact that a player might be benched, or even captained, factors which would greatly affect the calculation. And so, Effective Ownership (EO) was born.

Fix also introduced their own metric, Expected FPL Points (xFPL). In a nutshell, xFPL is calculated using Expected Goals (xG) and Expected Assists (xA), which combine as Fantasy Premier League (FPL) Involvements (xG + xA = xI). It also incorporates Expected Clean Sheets (xCS), appearance and bonus points. This metric translates these underlying statistics into an overall expected FPL point score (xFPL) and can be used to demonstrate when players have 'performed' well, even if their actual score was low.

2020

By 2020, Fix was growing arms, legs and tentacles. The company needed someone who could manage all the separate threads of the business, pulling them together and ensuring they worked harmoniously.

That's when they brought in Tom, the chap I would eventually meet.

It was in this year that the team at Fix decided to channel their energies into redeveloping the Fix mobile app, an element of the business which, for various reasons, had always proved problematic. This turned out to be worth the effort, as the powerful tools and features were no longer bound solely to the website, but could be accessed by users on the go via their smartphones.

2021

Fix now had over half a million users on their platform. OptiBot – the official name for the algorithm – had made over a billion squad optimisations since the company's inception. It was in this year that Fix created the Elite XI concept. The feelers went out to recruit eleven FPL managers with outstanding career histories. The idea being that Fix users would be able to follow the moves of some of the world's best FPL managers, tracking their transfer decisions in real time. If a manager who boasted 7 x Top 10k finishes changed their captaincy, users could know about it as soon as it happened.

MY RELATIONSHIP WITH FIX

It was at the beginning of the 2022/23 season that my story intertwined with Fix's continued expansion.

For those of you who have read my previous book, you will know that in 2021 I was struck down with a neurological issue which, amongst other things, affected my balance and ability to properly process what I was seeing. As someone who worked in the very hands-on construction industry, I was forced to leave my job – apparently walking around deep trenches and 21-tonne excavators is not recommended for someone who struggles to walk in a straight line!

During my recovery, I realised that if I was sitting still, my vision and balance were normal. Not content to be withering at home in front of the television, I poured all my energies into my main passion, writing. In two years, I published three books from my children's interactive fantasy series *Adventure Quest*, and my first work of non-fiction *FPL Obsessed: Tips for Success in Fantasy Premier League*.

With these books published and, thankfully, doing well, I needed to increase my income. Sticking with the theme of the written word, I became an Intermediate Member of the Chartered Institute of

Editing and Proofreading (CIEP) and retrained as a freelance copyeditor.

While I learned a lot during my training, I found the work came naturally to me and so the biggest challenge was not so much 'learning the ropes' but starting from nothing to build up a client base. This involved, initially, doing a lot of proofreading and editing for free in order to get my name out there and attract repeat business.

It was around this period that I had a chance encounter with Tom who, by now, had been with Fix for roughly a year. Tom contacted me out of the blue – as he had done with many active members of the FPL community – to ask if I would be willing to test and provide feedback on their new Google Chrome Extension,[2] which would merge Fix tools and data with the official FPL website interface.

With time on my hands, I gladly accepted and provided Tom with a detailed document highlighting what I liked, what I thought could be improved, and identifying any bugs or issues I had encountered (which, in truth, were very few). Tom seemed impressed with the feedback. He also mentioned that a former member of their development team,

---

[2] Something I still use to this day.

whom I knew from the FPL community, had spoken highly of me.

I decided to take the opportunity to ask if Fix needed anything in the way of content creation or editorial oversight. As it happened, the Fix team were looking to push the Elite XI: Team Reveal feature, and asked if I would be interested in writing weekly articles to introduce the individual Elite XI managers, focusing on their playing styles and the reasoning behind their decision-making. In effect, this would give the audience a deeper insight into how the minds of some of the world's greatest FPL managers actually worked.

As Tom was getting increasingly busy managing all the necessary relationships to keep Fix moving – not to mention marketing, content scheduling, customer service, troubleshooting and more – it was decided that they should take the management of the Fix Twitter account away from Tom and give it to someone else.

And so, with great delight, I accepted both positions and became a member of the Fantasy Football Fix team.

WHO ARE THE ELITE XI?

During the summer of 2022, FPL managers began eagerly awaiting the first nuggets of information from FPL Towers. When would they announce the player prices? Would they tease us with staggered player releases as they had done the previous season? Would they communicate their intentions beforehand? Members of the FPL community would compare dates from previous years as to when the game went live and extrapolate that information to predict this year's release date.

At this point, I was being introduced to a totally remote working environment with lots of moving parts. I was set up on Slack[3] – previously alien to me – and introduced to the Elite XI managers. My first thought was that there were 14 of them, not 11. At this Tom chuckles: "Yeah, well, it's good to have a bench."

I won't go into too much detail here about the individuals who make up the Elite XI – as this will be the focus of the next part of the book – but, as a light introduction, the Elite XI ("Elite XIV" doesn't have quite the same ring to it) are FPL players from all

---

[3] For those who don't know, Slack is a bit like WhatsApp but specialised for the workplace. It is a collaborative messenger program for online companies.

around the globe who can demonstrate a consistent history of excellent season finishes.

Between the 14 managers, they boast a staggering 82 x Top 10k finishes. That means the current roster of Elite XI managers average almost 6 x Top 10k finishes each. Of those 82 x Top 10k finishes, 61 of them are actually Top 5k finishes, and 18 of them are within the Top 1k. Our most colourful Elite XI manager, Craig,[4] boasts the best single overall rank of the lot, finishing 80th in the 2018/19 season.

Fix Premium users have unrestricted access to the Elite XI: Team Reveal area. Here, every Elite XI manager is listed. A brief bio gives a flavour of each individual's FPL playing style (covered in more detail in Part Two), their FPL career history and live rank.

Their current squad is also shown and, importantly, is kept up to date. The moment an Elite XI manager confirms a transfer or changes their captain, this is updated on the website in real time. Premium users can subscribe to managers' push notifications and/or email alerts and will be contacted directly should their selected manager(s) make any changes.

Chip usage, team value and the number of free transfers left are all shown alongside a Manager Mindset feature which displays notes, written by the

---

[4] We will meet him later!

Elite XI manager, explaining why they have made/intend to make certain moves, or notations on any chip strategies they may have formed.

Perhaps most powerful of all, is the Consensus XI feature. This shows the aggregated squad comprising the most-owned players from the Elite XI. In that sense, it displays the combined wisdom of some of the very best FPL managers on the planet.

WHAT IS THIS BOOK ABOUT?

My previous book was a guide to success in FPL. Success is, of course, as we define it. It was not written to tell you how to win FPL for two obvious reasons. Firstly, as someone who has never won FPL, I am no authority on that subject. Secondly, no one who has ever won FPL has ever won it a second time. Therefore, even an FPL winner is unable to emulate their former success. This makes sense given the number of variables at play.

I have always held the belief that a Top 100k finish in FPL is something to be proud of and requires hard work to achieve. I would say that, barring an unusual level of bad luck (covered later), if you stick to the principles outlined in my first book, you can attain somewhere around a Top 100k finish, even if you hit some major setbacks along the way.

Since my previous book was published, I have stayed true to the strategies outlined in it and have not finished outside the Top 100k.[5] It is a general guide to FPL, covering all bases and taken from my 19 years' experience playing this wonderful – albeit highly frustrating – game.

The book you are reading now is different. This book is an investigation into the mindset of a selection of

---

[5] Although, at the time of writing, I am coming to terms with the fact that this streak may be about to end!

managers who have consistently achieved outstanding ranks in their time playing FPL. It is divided into four parts.

This part (Part One) is an introduction to Fantasy Football Fix and some background to the Elite XI concept.

Part Two is presented as a few case studies, focusing on certain members of the Elite XI. While each member has his own very specific playing style, certain members have a definitive vibe which, to a certain extent, can be categorised. This part will take a deep dive into a selection of Elite XI team members and will say: "He plays FPL this way, and this is how he does it."

Part Three recognises that while there are multiple routes to repeated success – as demonstrated by Part Two – there exists a thread of commonality among the Elite XI. There are certain strategies and behaviours which most of the Elite XI share. Strategies which transcend their own unique way of playing. These important elements should be viewed as the backbone of their success, and hence it is important that we incorporate these elements into our own playing style.

The final part, Part Four, explores the mentality of our Elite XI managers. How do they overcome adversity to claw back good ranks? How do they cope with a bad Gameweek? What methods do they employ to deal with the pressure of being recognised as elite? How do they feel about the fact that hundreds of thousands of FPL managers have access to their every move?

I would love to sit here and say, once you have read this book, you will be racking up Top 10k finishes every year for the foreseeable future. But this would be a lie. A master carpenter can teach you everything they know, but that does not necessarily mean you will be able to build a beautiful log cabin from scratch.

This book can show you how a specific Elite XI manager plays the game, but the thing that underlies all the words in the book is a human instinct which is made up of vastly complex mental processes, all fed from years' worth of experience. This simply cannot be captured in circa 40,000 words. What I *can* tell you is that, by the end of this book, you will have a greater capacity to be a better FPL manager.

There is one other ferociously wild aspect which no amount of learning can tame. Whether you are looking to win your first mini-league, or aiming to join the ranks of the FPL elite, you are constantly at the mercy of our next topic: Lady Luck.

HOW MUCH OF FPL SUCCESS IS LUCK?

This is one of my favourite subjects when discussing FPL. There is no correct answer, yet it can generate the fiercest debates. My opinion is that luck is responsible for around 50% of FPL success, the rest being skill, self-discipline, game management, research etc. If you were to put a gun to my head and move me towards one end of the spectrum, I would probably not argue too much with a 60/40 split in favour of luck. Many disagree with me, which is totally fine.

One of the leading arguments for those in favour of skill being a more significant factor is this: *if luck is such a big factor, then how do you explain the existence of managers who consistently attain high ranks across multiple seasons? Surely the passage of time lessens the impact of luck.*

It's a good question, and one I have pondered often. Here I will try to counter that argument with basic logic.

The premise of this argument is that the mere existence of people who have consistently good finishes, over a long FPL career, negates the contribution of luck. I disagree.

Imagine a hypothetical game with 10 million players. Like FPL, it is split into 38 Gameweeks. But in this game, every player rolls ten dice each Gameweek.

[22]

The total sum of the dice is your Gameweek score. The worst you could roll is a 10. The best is 60. Like any luck-based game you would have, at the end of the 38 Gameweeks, those who had done well, those who did poorly, and everything in between.

Repeat this again for ten seasons.

What you would inevitably get would be a right old jumble of results. Most people would have a mixed season history. Some really big scores. Some really poor scores. Some average scores. But you would also get a select group of people who did better than everyone else over those ten seasons. The 'elite' players, if you will. Of course, you would also have the opposite, a select group of people who consistently did badly. Both these select groups would represent a minority, but they *would* exist.

What this proves is that the existence of people with near-immaculate FPL career histories doesn't negate luck as an important factor. The argument doesn't stack up logically. Correlation does not necessarily equal causation. As we have just proven, even in a game entirely luck-based, an elite group would emerge.

This does not in any way detract from those who are amongst the elite, because **both skill and luck** are necessary to consistently achieve high overall ranks. With all that said, I do believe – although I can't prove it mathematically – that the impact of luck diminishes with time, but it is certainly ever present.

I conducted a survey amongst the Elite XI managers on the subject of luck (see Appendix A). Of the 13 who responded, 69% said that they believed that the reason they had such a good FPL career history was a combination of both skill and luck.

When asked how much of a role luck plays in consistent FPL success, 62% answered more than 30%. Furthermore, 100% of the Elite XI said that they considered themselves to be good at recognising the difference between good/bad FPL choices and good/bad luck.

Another thing I have noticed – although this is just anecdotally, I have no evidence to back it up – is that FPL managers who have only been playing the game for a relatively small number of seasons tend to be less inclined to perceive luck as an important factor, particularly if those managers have done well in those seasons. This makes sense. If I were a relatively new FPL manager but one who had a really strong record, I wouldn't like to believe that luck played a major role. Admitting that would, by definition, detract from the contribution my skill made to the success I was celebrating.

Those who have played FPL for a longer period tend to have a more pragmatic view and are often more willing to accept the role luck plays. Ultimately, we would all like to blame our poor seasons on bad luck and our good seasons on our excellent FPL ability. But the world doesn't work like that. Luck is indiscriminate, in both directions.

In the 2020/21 season, I rarely left the warm embrace of the Top 50k rank tier. In that season, whenever I made a bad transfer, the rest of my team stepped up to ensure a green arrow. There were a number of occasions where I 'settled' for a player because I couldn't afford his more expensive counterpart, only for the cheaper option to score their first goal of the season, while the player I wanted blanked. I was (mostly) on the right side of the Covid postponements, while many of my rivals were getting shafted. It was a delightful season – in no small part because I had just released my first book on FPL, which lent my published work a certain credibility – but I have no doubt that I was incredibly fortunate too. If I am honest with myself, better FPL managers than I had significantly worse overall ranks that me that year.

Luck is a sliding scale

Sadly, the distinction between luck and skill isn't always clear, and it's probably more sensible to think of luck as being on a sliding scale.

"There's big luck and little luck," quips Elite XI manager Mark Mansfield. To take an example, it is always unlucky if one of your players gets injured, even more so if you have only just brought them in. But I would have a lot more sympathy for somebody bringing in a soon-to-be-injured Mo Salah than someone bringing in Reece James. The former is renowned for never being injured; the latter is renowned for being made of fibreglass. Yes, bad luck is involved in both instances, but there is also a poor skill element to one of the decisions.

Likewise, in the Covid-affected seasons, some players got shafted when they set their captain and vice-captain as two players from the same team. Fairly standard practice in an ordinary season, but this was playing with fire when fixtures were being postponed left, right and centre. Again, if you ended up without a captain due to sudden fixture postponements, no one will argue that this is bad fortune, but if your vice-captain was also reliant on the same fixture, then this is shooting yourself in the foot.

'Little luck', as Mark calls it, can be described as the bounce of the ball on the field. A poor shot which takes a deflection and goes in, the keeper wrong-footed. Your captain having a wonder-goal denied by some off-the-line defensive heroics. This is the stuff that we are all subject to and, over time, usually balances out.

'Big luck' is when poor decision-making, ignorance or human error leads to a positive outcome. You may encounter this often with your work colleagues. Colin from HR has left the captaincy on a premium striker because he hasn't been following the football news and is unaware that his striker has pulled up in training. The prognosis does not look good. The manager was categoric in the press conference; this injury will rule him out. Engaged managers rush to transfer this player out, or at the very least bench him. But not Colin. He has no idea this is even happening. Yet, lo and behold, the premium striker has made the starting XI come Saturday morning. Not only this, but he scores a hat-trick! Was the manager using the press conference to play mind games with the opponent? Did the injury just turn out to be much less severe than initially forecast? Who knows? Colin certainly doesn't. But he has just shot up through the ranks, probably laughing at the fact his mini-league rivals were stupid enough not to captain the best striker in the game.

FPL 'butterfly effect'

In a game where every decision has long-term repercussions, we must not narrow our focus of luck to merely the immediate Gameweek. Even the most seasoned FPL managers can fall into shortsightedness, whether it be evaluating the success of a transfer, or assessing the effectiveness of a points hit. The same can be true of luck.

A few seasons ago, I got really lucky from a poor decision I had made a few Gameweeks earlier. I can't remember the players involved in the earlier decision, but essentially it boiled down to the fact that my desired transfer combination was about to get impacted by price changes (the outgoing player was going down and the incoming player was going up). I had the exact money for a series of moves which would have culminated in me bringing in Lewis Dunk for Brighton's good run of fixtures (this was back in the Potter era, when Brighton were better at the back than going forward). Whatever it was, I didn't want to take the very small risk involved and ended up swallowing the price changes. When it came to executing my plan, I couldn't afford Dunk, my preferred choice. I settled instead for Adam Webster. He wasn't quite as assured of regular minutes as Dunk and also didn't have his defensive counterpart's goal threat from set pieces. I still wanted the Brighton cover, so I brought him in — I couldn't really afford to do anything else.

In the closing stages of the game, Webster scored (his first goal all season) and kept a clean sheet, whereas Dunk got booked. With bonus points firmly in Webster's pocket, I got 15 points to Dunk's 5-

pointer. In what turned out to be a low-scoring Gameweek, Webster really made the difference for me. My fat green arrow was not down to my genius differential option. It was sheer luck combined with poor management earlier on. Pure and simple.

As a season progresses, it gets more and more difficult to evaluate the impact of our former moves. Even those managers who are obsessed with analysing future permutations will get to the point that the future branches of their decision-making trees blur into the unknown. One of the worst impacts of the FPL butterfly effect I have seen in a while happened to one of our newest Elite XI managers, Andrew Neave (who you will meet in Part Four).

There is a joke amongst the Elite XI. As soon as you join, you'll have your first bad season. This isn't strictly true, but it has certainly happened before, for reasons which will be explored later on.

Andrew Neave, who hails from South Africa, was recruited to the Elite XI at the beginning of the 2023/24 season. He brought with him 7 x Top 10k finishes, his best ever finish being 589th in the 2016/17 season. Fresh from yet another excellent finish in the 2022/23 season (1,022[nd]) Andrew was brought in to replace one of the outgoing Elite XI managers. Little did he know, he was about to fall foul of the running joke.

Like many of us in the 2023/24 season, Andrew didn't get off to the best start. But any chance of an early recovery was hampered by a seemingly endless string of bad luck.

"It started in Gameweek 9, I think," Andrew recalls, "when Udogie got injured."

In Gameweek 10, Andrew carried on with his planned transfer of Phil Foden to Kaoru Mitoma. He also transferred in Gabriel for the injured Sven Botman, the former having a plum fixture against Sheffield United.

"I'd been holding on to Botman for a while as the news was mixed as to his recovery. In the end I brought in Gabriel, who then didn't play against Sheffield United, so instead he joined Udogie on the bench!"

Needing to address his defensive injury crisis, Andrew sold Udogie and brought in Kostas Tsimikas, only for Newcastle's Dan Burn to get injured. Andrew bit the bullet and immediately got rid of the recently acquired Burn, bringing in Arsenal's William Saliba. Then Mitoma, whom he had only just brought in, picked up an injury. Andrew dealt with this by swapping the now-injured Mitoma for Eberechi Eze in Gameweek 12. Only for Eze – you guessed it! – to pull up with an injury after just 48 minutes.

The problem for Andrew, of course, is that all this fire-fighting was distracting him from making the high-quality transfers which make the difference in a season.[6] Going back to our sliding scale, this level of injury is way beyond what is usual and has nothing to do with skill.

While we all may quibble about exactly how much of a role luck plays, it is important to acknowledge that it is a significant factor in FPL. Embracing this fact helps with many things. It keeps us grounded when things are going our way and it can calm us down when things are going badly wrong. It also makes it easier to stick to our core FPL principles and playing style – assuming we have developed them – even when they don't seem to be working.

---

[6] You may be pleased to learn that at the time of writing Andrew has enjoyed seven out of nine green arrows and has shot up the overall ranking table from 1.4m to 326k.

PART TWO

MEET THE ELITE

ELITE XI

When I first joined Fix in May 2022, I was introduced to the Elite XI via a Slack channel. I will confess to feeling a little intimidated by the experience. The sheer number of Top 1k finishes I was surrounded by made my solitary Top 3k finish in 2010 feel more than inadequate.

I had gone from being one of the best people I knew at FPL – bar my nemesis Dan, who would occasionally take me down a peg – to a member of an online community who made my own FPL obsession look like a mere passing fancy. Now I was stepping into a room with FPL giants.

I envisaged a scene where we were talking FPL and I spoke up with an opinion only to be laughed out of the room by a bunch of monocle-wearing aristocrats guffawing at my pitiful squad. But that couldn't have been further from the truth.

In reality, here was a bunch of really nice guys from all over the world. Different personalities, different playing styles, different opinions. If someone said they were interested in a particular player, some would agree, some would disagree, sometimes heartily, but never with any malice or condescension.

It did not take me long to realise that this bunch of managers are mortals just like you and me. They are FPL managers who love the game, despite its unique frustrations.

Like us, they obsess over their moves. Like us, they fret over whether they have made the correct decision after the deadline has gone. And, like us, they hide behind the sofa when a highly captained player they don't own bursts through the opposition's defensive lines. The only difference between me and these guys was an incredible rank history.

Once I'd comforted myself that the group consisted of fellow human beings, I interviewed them one by one. The idea was that we would release a series of pre-season blogs which painted a profile of certain Elite XI members.

Fix's vision for the Elite XI was much more than saying, "These guys are good, copy what they do and you will win your mini-leagues." They wanted their users to really get to know the Elite XI. Find out what made them tick, be able to understand their differences, and match their own playing style to the corresponding member(s).

I was amazed at how different these managers actually were from one another. Just as I have mentioned in my previous book that 'there is no universal winning formula', the same was precisely true here. These managers had vastly different ideas of how to play FPL, and they all had proven that their own playing style – no matter how different – was effective, over multiple seasons.

One such example blew my mind. No longer a member of the Elite XI, Niklas Zanden was as unusual an FPL Elite as one can possibly imagine.[7]

Risk-averse, calm, and cautious in his approach, Niklas is a professor of Management at the University of Gothenburg in Sweden. As a result of his academic discipline, Niklas is extremely proficient in gathering information, selecting the right people to listen to, and pulling together many strands of knowledge to build a cohesive picture. Indeed, it was his job to teach students exactly how to do this.

When I met him in spring 2022, Niklas had 4 x Top 5k finishes and had come closest of all the Elite XI to winning the whole thing, having finished 22nd globally in the 2016/17 campaign. A remarkable career. But what was truly amazing was that Niklas did not watch Premier League football. In fact, he didn't watch football at all! *Well then, he must have been really good at analysing statistics*, I hear you cry. Wrong!

---

[7] Niklas decided he wanted to step back from the limelight and get back to a more private enjoyment of the game.

Niklas did not use *any* data to make his FPL moves. I couldn't believe my ears. I was talking to someone with an unbelievable record, who was a mere 21 places off winning FPL in its entirety, yet didn't use stats *nor* the eye test. This is what he said to me in the interview:

"I don't watch football. I stumbled into Fantasy Premier League because one of my friends introduced me to it. I don't have time for watching football. My eye test is following the written updates on the live text. I don't crunch tables and I don't do stats; that makes me a bit different. But I listen to others that do numbers well and I listen to those who know more about football than me and I rely on their eye test instead."

While Niklas is no longer a member of the Elite XI team, his playing style sets the tone for the breadth and variety of FPL expertise which is present amongst the group.

In this part of the book, we delve individually into a select group of Elite XI players and focus on exactly how they play the game so well. For various reasons, I will not be focusing on all 14 members of the Elite XI. Primarily, this is for the simple reason that some of the members of the Elite XI would prefer to be kept out of the public eye, to the degree this book will reveal. Also, I felt it more efficient to categorise the playing styles rather than drill down to the level of the individual. I have therefore focused on four 'case studies' rather than each member.

MARK MANSFIELD

The Opportunist

STARTED PLAYING FPL: **2002/03**

PERSONAL BEST: **227th (2014/15)**

TOP 1K FINISHES: **2**

TOP 5K FINISHES: **6**

TOP 10K FINISHES: **7**

WORST RANK: **121k (2011/12)**

MARK

It is 26th January 2024, an hour before my scheduled Zoom interview with Elite XI manager Mark Mansfield, and the news has just dropped that Jürgen Klopp is to leave Liverpool Football Club at the end of the season.

I watched the announcement video twice, some small part of my brain hoping that this is just some clever AI deepfake video. Perhaps I have been rumbled in some way. But it is not April 1st, and this has come from Liverpool FC's official Twitter account. This isn't a joke.

My phone is going wild. The football community is abuzz with the news. I feel like I have been sucker punched. The forward-thinking part of my brain tries to peek into the future. It looks pretty bleak. The last thing I want to do right now is talk to a Manchester United fan. Fortunately for me, Mark is an absolute gentleman. He doesn't rub it in too much, but his Irish sense of humour breaks through the polite facade as he teases the advent of a post-Fergie era for Liverpool. It is not something I want to think about right now.

But abject disappointment must be put to one side for now. I have an hour's slot with FPL royalty,[8] and I

---

[8] Which turned into – almost ironically given the topic – 90 minutes of chat.

have a lot of questions for Mark. Of course, like all the Elite XI managers, I have spoken to Mark before, and have a good grasp of his playing style, but what I want out of this interview – as much as it is possible to achieve – is a blueprint for his success.

BACKGROUND

Born near Dublin in the eighties, Mark has always been a big fan of football, particularly the Premier League. I often wonder what it is like for Premier League-obsessed people who live outside the UK, but as someone who lived in Dublin for two years, I have a pretty good idea already of what life was like for Mark. It is no different from back home. In fact, if anything (dare I say it) people are more Premier League obsessed in Ireland than they are over this side of the water.

In the early to mid nineties, a younger Mark would collect football magazines such as *Shoot* and *Match*. A little later on, he and his friends discovered a very rudimentary form of FPL – called Football Fantasy – via the *Irish Independent* newspaper. Readers could register a weekly starting XI using three-digit codes which represented each Premier League player. Players were given a budget of £40 million to spend. Making changes involved calling a premium-rate phone number at a cost of 58p per minute.

Of course, you could just use the framework provided to make your own game between your friends, and this is exactly what Mark did.

Not being able to afford the newspaper themselves, Mark and his friends were reliant on their parents having an unused copy of the latest issue, which they could greedily squirrel away and bring back to the group to study. On occasion, when none of the parents came forth with a copy, desperate measures were sought, and they would knock on random houses asking the residents if they had a copy they would be willing to spare. "It's only page 13 we need," they would plead to their perplexed neighbours.

With no verifiable record of which player selections were submitted, the friendship group relied on the honesty of their fellow players. Honesty which Mark says was tested when Queens Park Rangers forward Danny Dichio scored a hat-trick in the opening game of the season. Rather suspiciously, most of the group gleefully announced that they had him in their football fantasy squad.

"No one had ever even heard of Danny Dichio, so I think there was a bit of cheating going on there," muses Mark.

FPL HISTORY AND PLAYING STYLE

Like me, Mark remembers playing FPL prior to the 2006/07 season. However – due either to email address changes or some website migration issue – Mark's recorded FPL history starts in 2006. Starting as he meant to go on, Mark finished 258th in the world.

What I find most extraordinary about Mark's FPL career is that in 18 (recorded) seasons, he has only finished outside the Top 100k once (and even then, ranked at 121k, he was only just outside), which is a remarkable achievement. In total Mark has 7 x Top 10k finishes and two of them are inside the Top 300, including his best ever finish of 227th in 2015.

One thing which stands out about Mark is his easy-paced and considered manner. He has this aura around him which bends time to his own liking. When you ask him a question, he takes a moment to fully digest it and prepare his response. As a result, his answers are always concise and well thought out. There is no babble with Mark.

The beauty of the Elite XI concept, as covered earlier, is that users can tailor their interaction between themselves and the Elite managers. Having push notifications for all 14 managers may be a little overwhelming, so instead users can choose a manager (or a few) who most resembles their own playing style.

Without wanting to upset the other Elite XI managers, I feel Mark is most aligned with my playing style and general FPL philosophy. Obviously, he is considerably better at FPL than I am, but when Mark gives his reasons for a particular transfer, or shares the logic behind his long-term planning, I nearly always find myself nodding along in agreement.

As I was trying to push thoughts of Klopp's departure out of my mind, it dawned on me that I had no idea what Mark did for a living, so that's where we started. I was in for a shock.

As it turns out, Mark has spent the last decade or so working as a solutions architect in the development of Android apps. Having spent a portion of his life living in London, Mark is well accustomed to the work-hard, play-hard world of financial services. He later decided that the pace of England's capital was faster than he wanted, and exchanged the humdrum of Canary Wharf for the slower-paced, more serene atmosphere of his home city.

The reason I was shocked about Mark's occupation is because he has a PhD in Machine Learning, specialising specifically in reinforcement learning.[9] It doesn't take a genius to work out that the logical and systematic approach needed for this line of work would lend itself directly to FPL decision-making.

But I found myself surprised. My opinion of Mark – from previous conversations and interactions with the other Elite XI managers – is that he is more of an eye-test, intuitive manager. He watches a lot of the matches, and his tactical knowledge of football is very impressive. I told him that I thought he would be more of a stats-based manager, with those credentials.

"I am a stats-based manager," he replies. "I just don't go on about it like the others."

I ask him why he isn't overtly enthusiastic about statistics. I point out that I very rarely see him put a stat forward in conversation.

"I find discussing stats in the context of FPL really boring. My line of work forces you to think in the abstract and this is how I like to think of FPL, almost philosophically. I play FPL because I enjoy it and it's fun, but there's nothing to debate about statistics, they just are."

Mark then continues to say that his favourite podcast is FPL Blackbox. The reason for this is that the stats

---

[9] Something he doesn't really talk about.

are analysed fairly, with no cherry-picking. The hosts, Az and Mark (Sutherns), present columns and columns of data, so they are not hiding anything in order to pursue a preconceived idea. He also likes the fact that the statistics are always contextualised in a footballing sense.

"The two guys on it know football. So, if they see a statistic, and it's a bit of an outlier, they'll go after it, and they'll say 'why is that?' and then they get back to the football. So, for me, that's the perfect mix of stats and football knowledge. They are thinking big picture, rather than going after the narrative."

When I first interviewed Mark back in the summer of 2022, he described himself to me as a 'flexible opportunist'. Another characteristic of Mark, and one that is shared by many who have achieved success, is his ability to explain complex things clearly and in comprehensible language. Often, Mark can be quite philosophical about FPL. When I ask him how he categorises himself in terms of playing style, his answer is short and simple.

"I will do whatever it takes to get points."

You may scoff at this and think, *well, yes, that's what we are all trying to do*. But when he says it, he really means it. I would articulate it this way: there is no stone Mark will leave unturned in the pursuit of gaining as many points as possible. This comes in two parts.

The first part is that Mark will acquire information from many, many sources to inform his FPL decisions. He listens to podcasts, he watches the games (and if he doesn't catch a game, he makes certain he catches the highlights), he trawls through the statistics, he fills any gaps in his knowledge by asking the right questions of the right people. In short, he lives and breathes FPL. When striving for success, many people go looking for the quick, easy answer. In most cases, success comes from hard work and dedication, not the press of a magic button.

The second part is that while we all may think we are trying to get as many points as possible, many of us are 'attached' to a certain way of playing. Many managers who are active in the Twitter community cultivate an online persona. There is an expectation from their followers that they will act in a certain way and they may be hesitant to deviate from that strategy, even if they feel it is the right thing to do. "That transfer wasn't like you," some might say. Mark, however, is firm in his conviction. He does not care one bit what people expect him to do. He has no expectation of himself, other than to maximise points. If you ever find yourself worrying about what others might think, Mark is living proof that this is a wasted line of thought.

What I noticed about Mark's playing style is that he is quite happy to adhere to the template, but only on the proviso that he agrees with the majority. He will then keep analysing the landscape and waiting for the time when the majority let an opportunity slip by. That's when he strikes.

"I always question *en masse* decisions. A lot of the time, they're fine. But sometimes I don't agree with where the masses are heading; that's when it can be good to jump on a player like Watkins, or Palmer, early and get the advantage."

This line of questioning leads to the oft controversial topic of Effective Ownership. I want to know if ownership statistics factor into his FPL making decisions. He grumbles slightly at the mention of it and shifts almost imperceptibly in his chair.

"I don't want to, but sometimes you kind of have to."

It is one of the great annoyances of FPL. While it would be wonderful to remain unaffected by what the masses are doing, the reality is that we are playing a game where success is governed by not just how we are doing, but how we are doing *relative to our opponents*. If it is a coin flip between two players, the more highly owned player will hurt us if we get it wrong. Yet the lesser-owned player will be the more fruitful of the options if we get it right. This all comes down to our appetite for risk and/or our current position in relation to our objectives.

I asked Mark to envisage a hypothetical situation in which he had just landed home after a trip to the wilderness, with no recollection of his squad or recent football knowledge. He powers up his laptop and looks at this FPL for the first time. What, I asked, is the process for deciding what to do next?

"Well, the very first thing I would do is set up my bus team (see Glossary). Is it amazing? If so, I would leave it and roll the transfer," he explains. "I'd also want to know do I have the best captain for that Gameweek." Mark then explains how he likes to own at least the two best captaincy options for any given Gameweek.

"Then it comes down to the simple question 'Is there a move I can make which leads to more points this Gameweek, and in the future?'"

I ask if he generally targets incoming or outgoing players first. He shrugs this off as inconsequential. Moving on to the fixture vs form debate, Mark becomes uncharacteristically animated. His eyes light up as he declares, "Fixtures over form, every time!" In case this wasn't clear enough, he adds, "Fixtures are king!"

Once these elements are established, the pool of candidates is somewhat narrowed. Then it is about refining the remaining options down to the best choice. At this stage, it is all about using statistics to find who has been exhibiting the most attacking threat.

Underprepared for the fact that Mark uses statistics as heavily as he does, I hadn't left much room in the interview to get into the nitty gritty of analysing the numbers. I was also aware that the numbers side of things would be taken care of courtesy of Corey Baker and James Cooper (read on for these case studies).

ELITE ADVICE

Coming to the end of our time, I asked Mark to offer two pieces of advice for anyone who wanted to take their FPL game to the next level.

"Never knee-jerk," he states categorically. "It is the biggest sin in FPL."

Mark is not averse to early transfers per se, but they should not be made out of anger or frustration. Being able to make your transfers with all the available information readily available is optimal, but he accepts there are those times when price changes are going to disrupt well-laid plans. If you are going early, then do it for the right reasons, not because you have lost your rag mid-Gameweek.

"I did it with Alvarez against Sheffield United and I was so annoyed with myself. I allowed myself to get caught up in the buzz and convinced myself that I needed him. I didn't, and I regretted it."

"Secondly, immerse yourself in information. Podcasts, blogs, articles, data, everything."

Curating and refining the available information is also critical. There is so much FPL-related stuff to digest out there that it is not just about trying to take it all in. It is distilling the information into a usable form. Separating the wheat from the chaff, so to speak. Those who don't have enough time to do this manually need to find a trusted source who will do it on their behalf and present it in a concise and clear manner.

We round off what has been an enjoyable FPL chat with some final thoughts. I ask Mark if there's anything he'd like to add and he takes this time to reflect on the way FPL has grown.

"There's just so much information available for casuals these days. With YouTube and all the different podcasts, a lot of the hard work is done by others and now you have lots of FPL managers making the same moves. The key to getting ahead is to go early on these players and make the gains before others do. If it is a weird sort of season, then being able to adapt to it will make a big difference."

Wise words from one of the best FPL managers out there.

JAMES COOPER

The Numbers Guy

STARTED PLAYING FPL: **2010/11**

PERSONAL BEST: **1,000th (2018/19)**

TOP 1K FINISHES: **1**

TOP 5K FINISHES: **5**

TOP 10K FINISHES: **7**

WORST RANK: **81k (2016/17)**

STATISTICS

I'm a big fan of consistency of structure in my books, but when it came to looking at the Elite XI member who falls under the statistics-loving category, I soon realised that I'd have to split this 'case study' into two parts. Having spent years interacting with both James Cooper and Corey Baker, it became clear to me that both guys loved their numbers. It would be difficult to choose between them, but something was happening this season which meant that perhaps I didn't have to.

You see, last season James Cooper beat all the other Elite XI managers, topping the exclusive league table and bagging yet another (his seventh) Top 10k finish with an overall rank of 6,420. Corey, on the other hand, finished near the bottom of the Elite XI league, by (almost) adding a zero onto James' finish. Corey had a rough season (by his own lofty standards) and finished 64,983. Still a respectable Top 100k finish – not to mention about 20k places above yours truly – but lower than he would have wanted.

This season, the reverse seems to be happening. James, at the time of writing, is currently rock bottom of the same league and has only just emerged from the Top 1m rank tier. Corey, on the other hand, is near the top and just outside the Top 100k mark. There's plenty of time to go – and both managers have all their chips still intact – but I find it interesting that the two managers who are most overtly into stats are having such polar opposite seasons.

I felt this was a good opportunity to see if this is down to different interpretations of the same data, or merely variance showing its influence on the game.

JAMES

James, originally from Yorkshire, has fond memories of visiting the (then) Reebok Stadium with his grandfather when he was just 11 years of age. When not watching Bolton Wanderers in action, his grandfather enjoyed doing the crossword puzzles in the newspaper. The rest of the paper would be surplus to requirements, and James would take great delight in finding the fantasy football pages. Like Mark, he would create his own teams using the provided codes. Unlike Mark, however, James once had to explain to his parents why he had dialled the premium rate phone number to register his first squad!

James cottoned on to FPL in the 2010/11 season when he registered his first online squad. In that season he finished 35,305. It was safe to say James was hooked. His earliest memories of FPL were desperately scouring the Liverpool fan forums to see if anyone could tell him if Sami Hyypiä was first choice in defence.

"Back in those days," James reflects, "it was all about trying to get the cheapest defender from the 'top four' you could." It didn't matter if it was a full back or a centre back. No one was thinking about defenders going forward and providing attacking returns. It was all about clean sheets.

Fast forward 14 years, and James and I are waiting for our Zoom call to connect. James now works in North London where he has lived for the past five years, having pursued a career as a barrister, specialising in divorce law.

"Being a lawyer forces me to think objectively," James tells me. "Being self-employed also means I can manage my own diary and spend my free time obsessing over my moves." Unlike Mark, James speaks quickly. He is concise and clear, but his mind moves at a very fast pace. I can't help but congratulate myself on the decision to record the interview, as my pen makes furious notes.

Having learned a little about James' background, I am keen to get stuck into the nitty gritty of his playing style. I start by outlining a huge conundrum I have with stats, which is how to decide the most effective time period within which to evaluate the data. The underlying rule of statistical analysis is the more data the better, but in the rapidly changing world of modern football – where Premier League managers change faster than UK prime ministers – player data is in danger of becoming less relevant. Player X may have fantastic xG from the previous season, but if he now plays in a more defensively minded system and gets fewer opportunities, is his historic xG as relevant?

"I think the biggest mistake everyone makes is not using a big enough sample size," James responds. "I remember reading an analysis a couple of years ago where they looked at xG versus goals and they were trying to work out how big a sample size you need in order for the underlying data to become accurate as a predictive tool, and they said 40 games."

He accepts that this is too long a sample size to use practically in FPL. "But it is illustrative of the fact that more is better." When picking his initial squad, James will look at all the data from last season and the seasons before. But he will then apply his footballing knowledge to it.

"If it's contextually relevant to do it, I will look at a narrower sample. If you know there's been a [tactical] change which could affect the data."

Another facet of James' use of stats is how it has affected his chip strategy. Previously, James, like many of us, would always try to save his Wildcard until as late as possible. But in recent years, he nearly always plays it around Gameweek 8. Having crunched some high-level season data, James came to the conclusion that this was the optimal time to use the game's most important chip.

"After eight Gameweeks, there is a reasonable correlation between the players who have the best underlying data at that point and at the end of the season. It's not super strong," he warns, "but it is strong enough that you have a good idea of what trajectory those players are on."

I find this interesting because I have my own private rule that I categorically will not play my Wildcard before the conclusion of Gameweek 6, as I believe that is the bare minimum of data required to make a sound judgement. Only in the – thankfully rare – event of total disaster will I consider playing it any earlier.

We get back to the conversation of evaluation of data periods. Later on in the season, James tends to stick to a period of eight Gameweeks or longer.

"When you look at a player's underlyings over four Gameweeks and see that they are good, this could be pure chance," he explains. "All it takes is for the player to have had one really good game – or taken a really good shot – and his xG for those games could be 1 or more. It could be pure chance, but it could also be important. It could be that they are now playing up front. All the footballing reasons that could be responsible for that difference, formation or personnel changes must be considered."

If you have read my first FPL book, you will know that I went through a period of my life where I painstakingly transposed statistics into my own spreadsheets to find out which players represented the best value. I ask James if he does anything similar.

"No, I don't put the information anywhere. I just look at the player, look at their numbers and the time period and then that just sticks in my head."

On the theme of interpreting data, I am curious as to how James avoids unconscious self-bias. I won't be unkind by mentioning specific names, but there are people in the FPL community who are renowned for 'cherry-picking' statistics in order to support an existing narrative, as opposed to being guided by the numbers in the purest sense.

James gives a knowing laugh. I know from previous conversations that manipulation of statistics in order to push already preconceived notions is something of a bugbear for him.

"I am quite a logical person anyway," he explains. "That ties in with being a lawyer. I have to be objective and systematic. If I'd decided on a pick and the numbers didn't support it, then I would reassess my view of the pick. More often than not, though, it is the numbers which inform the pick, not the other way around."

There are so many available statistics out there, right down to how many touches of the ball a player has taken in the opposition's box. I pose a question, which I hope will be tricky to answer. If you were about to lose all player data, bar three metrics, which ones would you 'save'? James answers quickly and assuredly.

"Non-penalty goals per 90," he answers, and then after a brief pause he laughs. "I don't think I need another one."

Knowing that I expect him to name two others, he looks up reflectively and adds Expected Assists (xA) and shot volume (total shots). But this comes with a caveat.

"It is interesting to cross reference non-penalty expected goals with shot volume. Because if someone is having fewer shots, then it's more likely that a good xG is simply variance in the underlying data. If someone is getting good shot volume and good xG regularly, then something is working in that system."

To illustrate an example, he mentions Everton's Abdoulaye Doucouré, who has had pretty good xG this season (at the time of writing) but is only averaging one shot per game. This extra level of variance makes James less assured that the trend will continue. While Doucouré's xG might look good in isolation, the low number of shots is a concern. This is a great example of how shot volume and xG go hand-in-hand to paint a more complete picture.

James also highlights that while he will also look at shots on target (as opposed to shots overall) it is probably less important to him as the relevance of that metric is, to a degree, already embedded within xG. This leads him onto what he describes as 'the big debate'; how good is a player at finishing? James believes that while there are a few exceptionally talented finishers – quickly citing Lionel Messi and, to a lesser degree, Son Heung-min – that 'great finishing' as a concept is overrated.

"If you look at the vast, vast, vast majority of player data, over a big enough sample, their expected goals will match their goal output. If you look at Salah over a five-year period, he hasn't scored any more than his expected goals."

James' mistrust of the concept of 'good and bad finishers' is backed up by the excellent book *The Expected Goals Philosophy* by James Tippett. In this book, the author downplays the importance of finishing, making the (perhaps controversial) claim that the vast majority of elite players have a similar ability to finish.

Tippett, like James, cites Messi as an obvious anomaly to this, and says that, in the overwhelming majority of cases, expected goals and actual goals come into line, given enough time. To the author, whether or not a high-quality chance is converted into a goal comes largely down to luck or variance. It is a player's ability to continually put themselves into the position to get those high-quality chances that we – and the broader footballing world – should be looking at.

While expected data and actual output generally come in line over a long enough period of time, there can be short-term pain involved in waiting for this equilibrium to occur. Owners of Nicolas Jackson and Darwin Núñez in the 2023/24 season will understand this all too well.

BEYOND STATS

Excited by the wealth of information James is giving me, I realise that we are running out of time and have been speaking almost exclusively about statistics. I fire some additional questions his way.

On the fixtures vs form debate, I wonder if James' proclivity to look at player performance data would mean that he errs on the side of the form. As it happens, the opposite is true. James favours fixtures over form, and by a considerable margin.[10]

"I am not totally sure form exists, whereas fixtures have been shown to be incredibly important to create better underlyings. If anything fixtures are underrated; home advantage is also underrated."

Digging deeper, I ask James why he doesn't think form exists.

"Form, in terms of goal scoring – as opposed to underlyings – I don't think really exists. I don't think someone scoring a goal makes them more likely to score a goal in the next week. Scoring three weeks in a row doesn't mean they are more likely to score in the fourth week. At least the data doesn't support

---

[10] It is worth mentioning that form, in this context, is considered to be recent player returns (goals, assists, FPL points) rather than the underlying data which leads to those returns – a player in good form from an FPL perspective is a player who has been returning FPL points.

that. Form, in terms of underlying data, exists to a degree, but there's usually a reason for this." And herein lies the need for footballing context once more.

With four minutes left, I fire off another one. Does Effective Ownership play a large role in your decision-making?

"Not a large role, but it does play a role. I tend to weigh it more heavily with captaincy." While James may consider it in terms of captaincy options, he doesn't let it influence his transfer decisions, although he does describe a particular scenario where this worked against him.

"Yaya Touré really hurt me one time. He was scoring a worldie or a direct free kick every single week. He was curling these ridiculous goals in week after week, and I didn't buy him. I was thinking 'there's got to be a slice of luck here which can't carry on', but it did." This, however, James insists, is the exception rather than the rule. In most cases, the underlying data can be trusted.

On chip strategy, James has a pretty straightforward answer – one that I am pleased to say matches my own.

"Free Hit [for] the big blank, [Second] Wildcard somewhere before the big double, Bench Boost the big double, and Triple Captain on the other double.

The Wildcard is the most valuable and the Triple Captain is the least valuable."

James goes on to describe how he believes that the Free Hit is the second most valuable, not for the points it generates that Gameweek but for the strategic value it offers.

"It enables you to do things you wouldn't normally do, and to maximise the amount of players in an upcoming double. Whereas if you didn't have the Free Hit to navigate the big blank, you'd have to do everything differently."

ELITE ADVICE

As with all the Elite XI members, I asked James to offer two pieces of advice to anyone who wants to go from being good to elite.

Interestingly, James strikes the same note as Mark, warning FPL managers about the dangers of knee-jerking.

"Even decent [FPL] managers are far too prone to being like 'Oh my god! That guy has scored a brace' or 'He's scored three times in a row, I must get him!' It may well be that someone who is scoring regularly is a good pick in terms of fixtures and underlyings, but it may not be. And just because someone has scored a brace and is going up in price, this shouldn't affect your squad planning."

Finally, James reiterates the importance of saving your chips to navigate the blank and double Gameweeks. He notes that many engaged managers will already do this, and with the recent meteoric rise in FPL content a lot of the hard work is done by others, but this is something which James feels is very important and worth repeating. He finishes off by pointing out that he always gets his biggest rank rises during this point of the season.

COREY BAKER

The Sports Data Guy

STARTED PLAYING FPL: **2012/13**

PERSONAL BEST: **897th (2014/15)**

TOP 1K FINISHES: **1**

TOP 5K FINISHES: **4**

TOP 10K FINISHES: **4**

WORST RANK: **125k (2013/14)**

COREY

It is 7pm on Sunday evening as I wait for Corey Baker to enter the Zoom call. Making this interview possible has required some negotiation with my wife, as I am usually putting our children to bed at this time. However, with the six-hour difference between us and the United States, this was the most mutually convenient time Corey and I could come up with.

From a work perspective, Corey has been an absolute lifesaver when it comes to writing the Elite XI articles. While our own playing styles are very different, Corey – aside from Craig, who we will meet a little later on – is probably the Elite XI manager I feel I know the best.

One of the challenges of doing what I do is the varying levels of engagement with the Elite XI guys. While they all make their squads available for the Elite XI: Team Reveal tool each week, some are naturally more active than others on the Slack channel. This, of course, is perfectly natural. Not everyone is glued to their computers all the time. Some people prefer to communicate via text, some are comfortable being recorded for video interviews and/or live streams, while others prefer to operate from the shadow of anonymity as much as possible.

I created a schedule at the beginning of the season so that I could cover each Elite XI manager on a sort of rolling basis throughout the season. Invariably, things change and people sometimes need to cancel. Whenever this happens, Corey – despite the time zone difference – is always on hand to fill in the gaps, often at the drop of a hat!

This is, in short, because Corey absolutely adores FPL. But it is more than just this. I think Corey's thoughts on FPL begin to back up in his brain like water being held back by a dam. He seems to find it cathartic to let these thoughts break free and flow into the world. He is very active on Slack and will often stream his real-time thoughts on a certain player pick or captaincy decision, always backed up by statistics, of course.

I sent each of the Elite XI managers I was interviewing a sheet with the questions I wanted to cover. My intention was not to have any form of rigid structure – as I find it much better to allow the conversation to play itself out – but to allow the interviewees to start to think about the answers ahead of the Zoom call. Corey, in true Corey style, edited the sheet with his answers and sent me pages of information, well before our scheduled meeting.

BACKGROUND

Originally a software engineer, Corey has spent most of his career in IT management. He lives in Chicago, Illinois, which, due to a quirk of international Premier League streaming rights, gives Corey a unique advantage when it comes to watching the action.

"We have this thing called Peacock, which is associated with NBCUniversal. Every [Premier League] game is live, but there are also replays. They [the replays] stick around for like six months, so if you want to go back and analyse games, you can."

Corey started playing FPL in 2012, the season after Manchester City won their famous title under Roberto Mancini, following one of the most exciting conclusions to a match in footballing history.[11] In his first season, Corey was less than 500 places away from a Top 10k finish. A difficult second season saw Corey finish outside the Top 100k – the only time this has happened in his career. In the 2014/15 season, Corey earned his best ever finish of 897. Back then, the appetite for Premier League football in the US was very limited.

"ESPN's website is like the bible of sporting events. But back in the day, they would rarely put anything on it [relating to the Premier League], but since then

---

[11] "Aguerrooooooo!"

it has grown and grown. NBC getting the sports package has really generated a lot of interest. It's kinda awesome to see!"

Corey points out that the short- and long-term physical danger of playing American football is becoming more apparent in the US, so consequently fewer and fewer children are entering the youth leagues and instead are heading towards 'soccer' as a replacement sport.

There is, of course, a major disadvantage to being an FPL enthusiast from the other side of the water. Time difference. This is an absolute killer when it comes to deadlines, especially in the modern era of FPL. I personally hate pre-deadline team leaks. I will try not to discuss them at length in this book other than to say they are a scourge on the game. But they have become an inevitable reality which we engaged managers can only ignore at our peril.

I like to lock in my transfers on a Friday evening so that when I wake up on Saturday, FPL can be about watching the games unfold and seeing the fruits (or lack thereof) of our decisions. Whenever I wake up on Saturday morning having not made my transfer(s) there is an instant tension in my head. Decisions still need to be made, data requires revisiting, transfer planning must be re-evaluated. All this when I should be spending time with my family. I can only imagine what this is like for Corey at 5am!

"Except in very unusual circumstances, I just don't worry about it any more," Corey explains with a sigh. "It's just not worth it. I hate this aspect of the game."

After a brief exchange of some notable incidents in our respective FPL careers,[12] I decide it's time to get down to the nitty gritty.

I very much want the focus of our remaining time to be on investigating the similarities or differences between the polarised results of Corey's and James' previous season (and the current trajectory of this season). I want to know if there is a divergence in the way he and James interpret the data, or if it is all down to the being on the right/wrong side of similar 50/50 decisions. Torn between steering the conversation this way, potentially biasing the results, and letting it flow naturally, I decide to be honest and inform Corey what I am trying to find out.

The first thing which becomes evident is Corey's use of a centralised system to analyse player data. Unlike James, who looks at the data and uses it to inform his decisions, Corey will log the player data in his

---

[12] Corey clearly remembers overtaking his mini-league rivals in Gameweek 38 courtesy of rare goals from Aymeric Laporte and Nathan Redmond. I brought up the time I nearly crashed the car when Aguero's fifth goal went in against Newcastle, widening the gap between me and my mini-league rival who had transferred him out that very Gameweek.

own colour-coded spreadsheet. This ties right into his occupation as a software engineer.

"I have created some code which will scrape FPL, uStat and FBref and pull the data down for both games and individuals. The code will then build spreadsheets automatically. It was super useful before xG data became readily available, because you couldn't just look this stuff up like you can nowadays."

While Corey can now get a lot of the core data from Fix's Opta Stats Sandbox and Customer Stat Builder tools, he still runs the batch files using his own code each Gameweek, a habit which goes back over a decade.

I ask Corey how he squares the 'recent data versus volume of data' argument, and herein lies another key difference between him and James.

"I only really look at the last six Gameweeks [of data]. I know the statistical purists will say things like 'you can't make a decision until you have like 12 weeks' worth of data' but that's just too long. You can't wait that long."

While Corey recognises that more data is preferred, he believes in being more aggressive when it comes to FPL analysis. This boils down to two reasons. First, waiting for three months before coming to any conclusions means a large chunk of the season has already passed. Second, reducing the data focal point means that any personnel or tactical changes which have occurred are far more likely to be excluded from the sample size and therefore non-relevant historic data is less likely to cloud the evaluation.

I decide to venture into uncharted mental waters (for me, at least!) and ask more about the data models he uses. I nod my head as he talks about a separate coding system (which, again, he created) he uses to rate teams. Using terms such as 'regression analysis' and 'statistical outliers', Corey discusses the importance of aggregating multiple sources of xG – because they are all subtly different – and how he improves his models each season.

While some – okay, a lot – of what he is saying goes over my head, I begin to realise that there is a fundamental rift between how he and James each capture and interpret underlying data. It is Corey himself who offers what is probably the key difference between the two statistical approaches.

"James actually disagrees with me a lot," explains Corey, "which I enjoy," he adds, smiling. He then continues to outline where their differences are and I am somewhat surprised by the answer, although it makes perfect sense.

To understand the different approaches, Corey believes we need to look at their respective backgrounds when it comes to the Premier League as a hobby.

"I didn't really grow up with the game, but I am a huge sports fan, not just soccer. I am probably one of the only Americans you will talk to who can tell you the rules of cricket or rugby. I watch almost all sports. But I didn't grow up playing the game because it wasn't popular where I live. So, I didn't end up watching it in any sort of analytical sense until I was in my early thirties."

As a result of this, Corey believes his ability to tactically analyse Premier League football doesn't compare to his nous for the more native sports, such as American football and basketball, which he grew up with. Compare this to James, who remembers watching Bolton Wanderers with his grandfather when he was just a small child, and we can see that the comparative immersion in football could well have led to huge differences in the way the two interpret the statistics.

As the discussion unfolds, I begin to get the impression that James is perhaps more naturally comfortable with his ability to analyse the game. While Corey watches a lot of different sports, James is probably more laser focused on Premier League football. As a result, Corey perhaps leans on data more, and is somewhat rigid in his approach statistically, whereas James is more willing to use the numbers to support his instinctive tactical knowledge. We see this in Corey's desire to limit historical data to iron out inconsistencies, whereas James gathers as much historic data as possible and then performs self-corrections based on his own knowledge.

This is not to say that either approach is wrong: James' way led him to success last season, and Corey is having the most joy this season. It is worth pointing out that, despite the increasingly obvious divergence in playing styles, a lot of the difference between their respective performances will also be at the inescapable mercy of luck.

With less than 20 minutes of our interview time left, I wanted to pose the same question to Corey about which metrics he would salvage if he were only allowed three. Top of his list was Non-Penalty Expected Goal Involvements Per 90 (NPGI/90). This is similar to James, although, whereas James looks specifically at Non-Penalty Expected Goals and uses Expected Assists as his secondary metric, Corey has compounded these metrics into the above. Both Corey and James agree on shot volume as an important metric, but for his 'extra' one, Corey adds Big Chances Created.

"I think what we need to be looking at is quality *and* quantity, right? And that's where the [shot] volume comes in. I get really nervous about players who have high quality but low quantity, because I feel like that's not sustainable. The more chances, the better."

ELITE ADVICE

As before, I ask Corey for the most important piece of advice he would give somebody who wanted to raise their FPL game to the elite level. In his notes, he has written: *plan for more than a single Gameweek, but not too far. Anything beyond six Gameweeks is unnecessary, except in extreme circumstances. But you do need to plan for a window.*

I find this interesting because I used to plan for a block of eight Gameweeks, but in more recent seasons – say the last three or four – I have found that I have naturally reduced this planning horizon to a maximum of six, and sometimes fewer. For me, intended plans don't tend to carry any further than that. Corey agrees.

"Typically my four-Gameweek window is where I am super focused and then I have kind of an idea what might happen [two Gameweeks beyond that]. After that, there's just too much going on. There's so many more games now, and so many injuries it seems. You've got to stay flexible."

A lot of this, we concluded, is a hangover from the Covid-affected era of Premier League history. Those who planned way ahead were severely disadvantaged by the fixture chaos and random postponements. If you were working on an eight-

Gameweek horizon, you would often find your team in tatters by the time you got to the end of it.

His next piece of advice relates to interpretation of underlying data. Specifically, Corey advises: "Learn how underlying data relates to on-field performance. Soccer is a low-scoring game so you cannot judge players simply on goals; there is too much statistical noise involved. That is where xG helps so much. But you have to understand the limits of xG and also the performance of individual models. Unfortunately, xG is a catch-all term for player modelling and yet they are not all alike."

Goals are so few and far between in football – especially when you compare it to other high-scoring sports such as basketball, cricket or baseball – that it is almost impossible to harvest useful conclusions using that metric in isolation. Corey elaborates:

"I mean, how many times have you seen someone score because they've absolutely shanked the shot? If they'd have hit it cleanly, then it probably gets saved. It's just so random, you've got to find another way to evaluate performance."

We finish off the interview reflecting on the difficulty of explaining xG to people who don't get it – or don't *want* to get it, as is often the case! Corey draws comparisons to the pushback received by Bill

James[13] and how the concepts get gradually accepted and brought into mainstream thinking.

This line of thinking naturally leads to the conclusion that as expected data becomes more regularly used – added to the recent explosion of FPL podcasts – the 'edge' that statistical analysts once had has become somewhat diluted. I asked Corey what he was doing about this.

"It's definitely more challenging. In the past, there would be players who would be scoring at an unsustainable rate. I would swerve them, but the masses would pick them up and get burned. But those days are gone. There are so many content producers out there, just like what we are doing with Fix, but many others too, and they are mostly offering solid advice.

"To counteract it, I am trying to be less 'punty'. In the old days, I used to enjoy taking the odd chance, but now I am more likely to wait until I have a solid base before taking any risks. So, what happened last year [in his poor season] I was up and down and then we broke up for the winter World Cup and so my base was never really there."

---

[13] The American statistician who revolutionised baseball as portrayed in the excellent film *Moneyball*.

He cringes as he recalls taking a punt on Chelsea's João Félix instead of Ollie Watkins, which was one of many decisions which derailed his season. This season, he feels much more disciplined. Hovering around the 80k mark (at the time of writing), Corey feels that he is playing more in keeping with his own style and, aside from an unsuccessful punt on Nicolas Jackson at the beginning of the season, he feels he has been focused on high-value, low-risk picks.

I pick up on the Nicolas Jackson transfer (mainly because I made the same mistake) and point out that the underlying data supported him as a pick, even though his goal output was massively below his expected stats.[14] Corey agrees, and the discussion unlocks the memory of a change he has made this season.

"Actually, one thing I have been doing this season is starting to incorporate finishing skill, just a bit. It's hard to quantify, but I do think we are starting to see certain players who are consistently good, or consistently bad, at finishing. It takes time, but I think

---

[14] Between Gameweeks 1 and 6, when Chelsea had incredibly generous fixtures, Jackson scored just once from an xG of 4.41 (the highest of any player except Manchester City's Erling Haaland) and 19 shots.

with some players you can factor that into your projections."

This is an interesting place to end the interview, because it shows that Corey is willing to evaluate a defined process and update it if he feels it is lacking in an area.[15] This constant self-correction seems to be a common thread amongst the Elite XI. Never standing still, they are not stubborn or arrogant enough to assume that the tried and tested methods of the past will always work. Much like his work as a software engineer, Corey understands the importance of not making wholesale changes to a working system, but ensuring he continues to make tweaks which add value.

---

[15] It also highlights yet another difference between his and James' perception of football, the latter believing finishing skill is largely exaggerated.

FPL ELITE: HOW TO BE THE BEST AT FANTASY PREMIER LEAGUE

CRAIG REUMERT

The Renegade

STARTED PLAYING FPL: **2007/08**

PERSONAL BEST: **80th (2018/19)**

TOP 1K FINISHES: **1**

TOP 5K FINISHES: **4**

TOP 10K FINISHES: **6**

WORST RANK: **494k (2013/14)**

CRAIG

Feeling a bit under the weather on a particularly wet and dreary Monday evening, I wait for Craig to join my Zoom meeting while I slurp a Lemsip and fight the urge to go straight to bed. Under normal circumstances I would probably have postponed the meeting as even the simple task of thinking feels a bit like wading through treacle. I put this thought out of my mind, however, as this is our third attempt to have this conversation.

The first was a little over three weeks previous. We had scheduled a time to catch up, but as I logged in to send over the video stream details, I received a message from Craig, which read:

Would you care to guess what day this is? It's our wedding anniversary. Nope. I didn't know that either. But apparently it is, so we may have to make it another night this week.

I laughed at the word 'may' and told him to go and dig himself out of trouble with his wife (on the express condition that I can use this as an anecdote in the book!).

The second attempt was a week later but, sadly, the reason for this cancellation wasn't in any way amusing. Craig lives in Copenhagen, working in procurement and facilities management. Our meeting was scheduled for 16th April 2024. This was the day that one of Copenhagen's most historically and culturally important landmarks, the old stock exchange building, became engulfed by fire. For Danes, this incident was on a similar level of tragedy to the Parisians who were forced to watch the Notre-Dame Cathedral burn back in 2019.

The building where Craig works is literally next door to the stock exchange building and hence his day had been both physically and emotionally draining. Craig had taken a client up to the roof of the building just the week before and took some pictures. On the day of our rescheduled Zoom, he sent me what may be the very last photos taken of the stock exchange building undamaged by the fire.

So, nearly a fortnight later, we were finally here. I must confess to being a little confused as to where Craig is from. I had assumed that he was Danish but couldn't shake the feeling that he had some connection to the UK, possibly London. I decided to clear this up early doors and ask him.

As it turns out, Craig is from South Yorkshire and moved to Denmark 17 years ago. This made a lot of sense. In particular, because Craig has a savage and direct sense of humour typical of that region. He also supports Sheffield Wednesday, which is another clue as to his heritage. His accent has undergone subtle changes over the years, which is one of the things which threw me. Especially since Scandinavians are renowned for being excellent English speakers.

Craig is in good spirits, after a very successful Gameweek 35, and enters the chat with a wide grin. Many FPL players have earmarked this week to play their second Wildcard and take advantage of the season run in, which happens to be peppered with a number of small double Gameweeks. Craig has been fearing this Gameweek, as the huge number of Wildcarders threatens his position. But he needn't have worried. Craig bagged 103 points, earning him one of the best Gameweek ranks I have ever seen (108th in the world) and boosting him from 150k to 41k in a single Gameweek.

BACKGROUND

Like so many FPL veterans, Craig remembers the fantasy football days which preceded the online game. He remembers that the *Guardian* newspaper ran their own version, which was heavily geared around price changes. Craig became obsessed with building team value, a trait which – to a degree – has followed into his FPL style.

I tell Craig that, rightly or wrongly, I view him as something of an FPL maverick, with a playing style which edges towards the aggressive. I ask him if this is a fair assessment.

"I wish I still was [aggressive]. It's funny you mention that because I used to be much more aggressive than I am now. I feel like I have lost my way a little by being together with these data-driven, slow-and-steady Eddies. A lot of the other managers don't take risks and they just grind it out and end up in the Top 1k every bloody season!"

I find this fascinating, as Craig is notably more aggressive than the other Elite XI members. The thought of him being even more of a renegade in the past is quite remarkable.

Despite any preconceptions this style of play may conjure up, Craig is also an avid planner and always looks carefully at fixtures. He breaks the season into blocks and seeks to maximise points over a set timeframe. He has no problems taking points hits to ensure he owns a key player during what he sees as an optimal period of the season.

"I like to think ahead. At any given time, I could probably tell you which moves I will be most likely to make, five or six weeks in advance. I always have an idea about what I am going to do. That's not to say I can't be swayed, but I am definitely fixtures over form."

In terms of his appetite for risk, Craig points out that it depends how you define a risk in the first place. Using hits as an example, Craig accepts that many managers perceive hit-taking as a risky business, but he illustrates that if your playing style involves targeting larger periods of time – as his does – then the chance of making good on your investment increases.

"Some people would see taking a hit as a risk, but if I am targeting someone for a six-week block and I think they are going to outscore the person they are replacing by 20 points, then that to me is not a risk – it's a no-brainer! In fact, the risk is actually not taking the hit."

As the conversation evolves, we get into a chat about the rise of online FPL content. Craig mentions the increased use of AI-based prediction algorithms, of which there are many available. This is another aspect of Craig's playing style I would like to know about. Of all the Fix managers, Craig seems to speak most often about AI recommendations, so I take the opportunity to ask him about the importance of AI in FPL decision-making.

"Well, first of all, it's a time saver. Since I had kids, my time available to research FPL has been reduced. But, more importantly, it's consistent, it's objective, and it's free from human emotion. I use it as a second opinion every week, just to see if there's some combination of moves which I haven't thought about. But it's also not something to be used slavishly. I can't think of an occasion where I have ever gone ahead with either of the first two recommendations which the model has given me."

Craig comes across as a little surprised that I have identified him as someone who uses the AI models more, as he considers it to be merely part of a larger repertoire of decision-making factors. He explains how he customises the parameters of any AI model he uses so that it fits in with his own style.

"I do also use it quite aggressively insofar as I use my own pejorative opinions to force it. Sometimes there are players [the algorithm recommends] where I am like 'Nah, I'm not having that, I don't want him anywhere near my team' and so I'll deliberately exclude those players from the model."

We then go on to talk about tweaking the AI to 'force exclude' or 'force include' certain players. This topic then segues neatly into a conversation about EO. If you were to plot Craig's average overall rank (within a season) on a graph, you would find it was much more full of peaks and troughs than any of the other Elite XI managers, whose graphs would show a much smoother incline. This is the same if you look at Craig's career history as a whole. For this reason, Craig says, analysing EO is a crucial part of his game plan, and he offers an example from the 2023/24 season:

"I was trying to find a way to bring in both [Alexander] Isak and [Anthony] Gordon, but I couldn't seem to make it happen. A big part of this was that the AI was insistent on putting in Son [Heung-min]. Now, I get that, because the AI model is only interested in getting the best possible score, so it doesn't consider ownership. But I take no joy in finishing 200k so, for me to get where I need to be, Son just isn't any good, because I knew everyone either owned him already or was going to Wildcard him in."

As it happened, Craig went for Kevin De Bruyne over Son, a decision which earned him four points net. I find it fascinating that Craig tweaks the algorithm to the extent he does. One may argue the futility of forcing the algorithm's recommendation to fit in with preconceived biases, but this is the difference between using AI as an augmentation to your decision-making processes, as opposed to just blindly doing what it says, despite your own misgivings.

ELITE ADVICE

I finish the conversation by asking Craig what advice he would give to anyone wishing to up their game to the next level and become an elite manager. I give the example of someone who is generally hovering around the 100k mark, who wants to take their game one step further.

"Well, first of all, when we are talking about achieving a 100k finish in a game with over 10 million players, we probably need to re-assess what we mean by 'elite level'. I mean, I forget how many Top 10k finishes I've got[16] but some of those were in years when there were only one and a half million players. Back then there were no podcasts, there wasn't the level of information available. It is much, much harder now."

This is a very good point and worth considering when we set our aspirations to the elite level. When it comes to a singular piece of advice, Craig struggles to put together a snappy answer. He explains how he thinks a more patient 'all-round' style (such as Mark's) may be the key to longer-term success, rather than his own aggressive style which yields more polarised results and a less stable rank journey within a season. Craig recognises that luck also plays

---

[16] It's six. And three of those are Top 5k, one of them is Top 1k.

a major part in obtaining an elite rank. Finally, he settles on this piece of advice.

"I've heard a lot of people saying, 'Just take it one Gameweek at a time' and I think that is rubbish. FPL is like playing chess. It's always about being a few moves ahead. You won't necessarily end up moving the pieces there when the time comes, but at least you've got the options laid out in your head and the flexibility to respond. And that requires, these days, to be at the top of your game to understand the data. Finally, understanding your own style and the way you like to play the game and following that rather than what anyone else says."

PART THREE

COMMON ELITE TRAITS

As I write this, I am currently ranked 779k in the world with just eight Gameweeks left to avoid my worst ever overall finish in nearly two decades of playing FPL. It is safe to say the 2023/24 season has been a complete and utter disaster for me.

Gameweek 29 has just seen my Free Hit chip slide down the drain into the unseen depths of fantasy football misery. Just 21 points between my 11 starters makes this one of the most underwhelming chips I have ever played. I knew I was in trouble within nine minutes of the football kicking off. Burnley vs Brentford was the first of just four fixtures in a weekend dominated by the FA Cup Quarter Finals.[17]

Having seen that Sergio Reguilón had been passed fit for the fixture in Friday's press conference, I made a last-minute tweak to my Free Hit squad, switching out Mads Roerslev for the more attacking Reguilón. In the fifth minute of the game, VAR decided to check an aggressive challenge by Reguilón on Vitinho, which the referee had totally missed. After what seemed like an eternity, a penalty was awarded to Burnley and Reguilón was shown a straight red card. Bruun Larsen stepped up to the spot and converted his penalty, wiping out Flekken's clean sheet. What's more, Ivan Toney, who blanked, also

---

[17] In which Liverpool were knocked out by Manchester United, to add insult to injury.

got booked in injury time, meaning that my three Brentford players scored a combined total of 0 points, Reguilón's -3 totally negating the scraps I received from the other two. This Free Hit was going, much like the rest of my season, down the toilet!

I am very glad of the international break, which will provide a brief respite from the seemingly endless pain of this season. But it also provides an opportunity to self-reflect on what has gone wrong. In the same way that a fantastic season is a combination of shrewd moves and good fortune, a terrible season is a combination of bad luck and poor decision-making. I decided to have a good look at where things had gone badly for me and try to sort the wheat (poor decision-making which can be learned from) from the chaff (mere misfortune which we have no control over).

A friend of mine in the FPL community used my FPL ID to run an analysis through an algorithm, which I don't fully understand. Apparently it measures actual points against expected points, using underlying data. (I'm sure there's more to it than that, but I think that is the gist of it.) The data revealed that not only have I been unfortunate, but I am in the bottom percentile of luck. Assuming you agree with the calculation provided, that means that for every 100 FPL managers, 99 of them have been more fortunate than I have.

But I am not willing to accept that my low rank is solely due to unavoidable variance. I instinctively know that I have also played badly this season. It's time to look deep into the mirror and find out what happened.

What went wrong?

Straight away, one glaring error jumps out, mainly because it has been uncomfortably festering in the background all season. This season, I have been guilty of 'premium hopping', particularly in midfield. I am usually incredibly patient with my transfer choices and very rarely transfer out a player who is doing well, even if that means foregoing a good opportunity. But this season, that has not been the case.

In Gameweek 5 I brought in Son Heung-min after his hard-to-ignore hat-trick against Burnley the previous Gameweek. With a game against newly promoted Sheffield United up next, this was a no-brainer. Of course, he blanked in that game. At this point, no major error had been made. You could argue that it would have been wise to have Son in *before* the Burnley game, two back-to-back fixtures against newly promoted sides offering a ripe opportunity for a haul. Those who brought him in early captured his hat-trick, which would have made the blank against Sheffield United more palatable. But I don't regret that decision, because, in all honesty, Son hadn't been playing well, and his underlying numbers didn't justify the inclusion of a premium midfielder.

The major error came next, when I transferred out Son immediately after in Gameweek 6. This wasn't a rage transfer. Spurs were about to face Arsenal and Liverpool, the former away from home. So there was at least a fixture justification for the move. The trouble is, I cannot win this argument. If I didn't like the fixtures in Gameweeks 6 and 7, then I shouldn't have brought him in for Gameweek 5. Conversely, if I really thought Son was a good pick, I should have kept him through the difficult fixtures, knowing good fixtures were on the horizon (Luton, Fulham and Crystal Palace were coming up after the Liverpool fixture). Whichever way you look at it, my decision-making was poor. I am guilty of either short-term planning or knee-jerking.

So, of course, Son went on to get six goal involvements in the next five Gameweeks. What about the player I brought in? It was Bryan Mbeumo, who blanked in the next three.

Not content with making this mistake once, I repeated it later on in the season.

In Gameweek 24, I swapped the ever-reliable and constant returner of points, Bukayo Saka – who had been in my team since the very beginning – for the newly-returned-from-injury Kevin De Bruyne, who had sent shockwaves through the FPL community by bagging a 12-pointer in just 21 minutes when he came on in the second half against Newcastle.

With a bold return from injury, and an upcoming double Gameweek for Manchester City, De Bruyne became an absolute must-have midfielder and was being raved about in the FPL community. I knew deep down that he was a 'minutes risk' due to the triple whammy of Pep Roulette, De Bruyne's recent return from injury and his age. But still I fell for it; hook, line and sinker.

In his next five appearances, De Bruyne scored just eight points (1.6 per game on average). In that same time period – and having played one less fixture – Saka scored 47 points (11.75 per game on average). When you factor in the -4 hit I took to make this change, then this decision alone cost me 43 points. At this stage of the season, this was equivalent to about 400k in overall rank. It is possibly one of the most damaging transfers I have ever made.

It is worth pointing out that this was *both* a skill *and* a luck issue. The skill issue was the decision itself, which was objectively and categorically bad. The luck issue was the intensity of the punishment. Saka had achieved six double-digit hauls all season and half of them had been in this small window. I had kept Saka due to his constant stream of small returns, but he hadn't really been an exciting, point-hauling choice.

Of course, this all changed the moment I transferred him out.

So, having assessed **what** damage occurred, I need to look at the **why** and then move on to **how** I can fix this error going forward.

Why did I let this happen?

I think there were two forces at play with both of these decisions. Firstly, I had no fires to put out. As Morrissey reminds us, the devil makes work for idle hands to do. This is one of those odd scenarios where I probably got *unlucky* by not having any squad issues. Had I been suffering from injury problems I would almost certainly have made 'boring' transfers to correct them rather than hopping from midfielder to midfielder and dodging points in the most spectacular way.

Secondly, I gave in to fear of missing out (FOMO). In both cases, the damaging transfers were focused on who I was bringing in rather than on who I was retaining.

How can I stop this from happening again?

The first step to fixing an error is to understand what has happened and why. But, in a game so full of temptations – embedded in a community so full of noise and opinion – it requires more than simply knowing what the problem is. It requires self-discipline, awareness and willpower.

On the first point, I cannot *make* my own players get injured simply to divert me from dangerous distractions, nor would that be a sensible thing to do if I could. But, if next season I have no fires to put out, I need to give a lot more thought to who I am bringing in and, crucially, who will be making way.

As I mentioned above, the decision to remove Son was largely justified by his next two fixtures (Arsenal and Liverpool). Yes, these fixtures are about as difficult as they get, but the ones beyond were very appealing.[18]

Perhaps, instead of tinkering, I could have burned a transfer (sacrilege!). Or made a very boring sideways move on my goalkeeper or third bench spot. Sometimes you find there is nobody in your squad you really want to get rid of, in which case the answer often is, well, don't.

The second point can be hard to remedy. How do we shut out FOMO? What can start off as a small desire in our heads will eventually become amplified once we see agreement from others. What started as "Maybe I should get Kevin De Bruyne?" soon became "I absolutely must get Kevin De Bruyne!" All that

---

[18] There is also the fact that the North London Derby is usually a high-scoring affair, despite the fixture difficulty.

changed in the interim was the fact that everybody was going on about him.

I even had a few warning shots fired across my bow. I literally had people cautioning me about the dangers of getting rid of Saka. One such warning came from one of the Elite XI members I trust the most (Mark Mansfield)[19] who said, and I quote, "This to me looks a bit like you are chasing double Gameweek players instead of chasing points." I should have listened, but I had become invested too much in the idea of owning the Belgian.

The easy answer to this would be to totally come away from the online FPL community so that I am not exposed to groupthink opinions, which can cause FOMO, although this feels a bit like using a sledgehammer to crack a nut. It also means losing out on the innumerable benefits of being part of the online community.

If you have this same conundrum, then a good compromise is to regulate your intake of information. Stop listening to 'the crowd', especially when it consists of people whose playing styles you are unfamiliar with. Curate your online experience and narrow down the points of view to people you

---

[19] This is not to say that I find the others less trustworthy, just that Mark's FPL philosophy feels closely aligned with my own.

trust. This is what I will be working on for what remains of this season and in the 2024/25 season (more on this later).

Forgive the aside. I wrote this both because it has been quite cathartic to do so (sorry, dear reader, for using you as mental health therapy!) but also to illustrate an important point. Honest and humble self-evaluation is critical to avoiding the same mistakes again and again. This is something which I have learned from the Elite XI and must emulate going forward.

ELITE COMMON TRAITS

In Part Two, we got a taste of just how different the playing styles of our Elite XI managers really are. If we were to look at all 14 managers in greater depth, we would discover that the differences between them are broader still. While this would undoubtedly prove interesting, the practical knowledge to be gleaned from such an endeavour would be minimal. In all likelihood, the more Elite XI managers we looked at, the more seemingly contradictory advice we would have to sift through.

But there are a number of aspects which all – or at least most – of the Elite XI share. These threads of commonality are critically important. If there is something which the world's best managers are all doing – despite their different playing styles – then it is obviously something which is worth doing. This section of the book explores the shared traits of the Elite XI. If you find yourself lacking in any of these areas, then these are the aspects you should prioritise on your journey to becoming elite.

1. PLAN AHEAD

If I could only choose one singular aspect of FPL strategy which the Elite XI share, then the capacity for effective forward planning is the one which jumps out the most. It doesn't matter if you use statistics as your main guide, or if you have a more intuitive approach to FPL. Whether you look at recent form, or the upcoming fixtures. The ability to plan ahead effectively serves as the core principle that binds all our elite managers together.

But how far ahead should we plan?

According to a survey conducted amongst our Elite XI managers, 78% look ahead to a time horizon of between 5 and 6 Gameweeks. None of our managers look beyond that. The remaining 22% are more short-term, looking at 3-4 Gameweeks. None of our managers look at a time frame shorter than that.

This means that, for most of our managers, a transfer pick has to still offer good value at least five Gameweeks down the line. Adherence to this discipline means that our Elite XI are less susceptible to short-term fads and/or FOMO.

The major practical benefit of planning ahead to this degree is that your squad should always be one step ahead of the times. People who only look ahead to the next Gameweek can suddenly find themselves in a situation where a significant proportion of their squad is about to enter a difficult period of fixtures. They may have made decent short-term gains by always having the 'best' player for each particular Gameweek, but this unsustainable practice will eventually lead to a point where any gains made will soon be undone by either a) having to weather a difficult patch, b) using hits to fix the squad, or c) playing chips early in order to navigate an avoidable problem.

Those who have planned ahead well can layer their squad with short, medium and long-term holds. Managers utilising this method will be able to identify players who are about to head into a rough patch of fixtures as their outgoing transfers. Their replacements will be players who are about to embark on a good run for the foreseeable future. The medium-term holds will soon be coming to the end of their good run, but not just yet. They will provide a smooth transition over the next few Gameweeks, until they become the next players who will require attention, and so the process repeats. This means the squad will always be in a healthy position, barring any unforeseen events such as injury, management changes etc.

But forward planning goes deeper than this. There is no sense in planning to bring in Player X in Gameweek 10, with Player Y making way, and then discovering that you don't have the budget to make this transaction a reality. Those who plan ahead effectively will know in Gameweek 5 that there is a good chance they will want to bring in Player X in Gameweek 10. Logic follows that in Gameweek 4 they will have an idea of whom to get in Gameweek 9 and so on. Following this path enables managers to check that their planned transfer path is viable in terms of budget and any other constraints (having too many players from the same team, for example).

Deeper still, planning ahead is essential for identifying future information which will have a bearing on current decisions. Non-Premier League fixtures – such as domestic cup ties or European games – may fall within the time period being analysed. These factors could have a bearing on rotation or fitness levels. Perhaps one of the players who is about to go into a good fixture run will have that run interrupted because they are taking part in AFCON or the Asian Cup. Failure to identify these upcoming possibilities can lead to erroneous short-term decisions which require correcting later on.

This is all without even mentioning blank and double Gameweek planning, which is the period of the season where the most dramatic points totals can be realised and when the most significant rank swings occur.

Detractors of forward planning in FPL tend to use the same argument: FPL is a rapidly changing landscape, therefore your planned transfers in six Gameweeks' time are unlikely to happen. That being the case, why bother looking that far ahead?

It is a fair question, and the preceding statement is correct. It is rare indeed that a transfer planned that far in advance actually goes ahead. So why bother making the plan?

To start with the most simple answer: things do sometimes go as planned. You may have a period in which your squad suffers no injuries and no new ground-breaking information emerges. In which case, great! You can follow your pre-planned transfer and captaincy path.

But let's say, as is likely, things happen which force you to deviate from your path. All you need to do is amend the current plan. This is much easier than creating a new plan from scratch. The foundation of planning has already been set and the principles those future transfers are based on still hold true.

Let's say Liverpool are about to come into a really good run of fixtures in five Gameweeks' time. You plan to bring in Trent Alexander-Arnold for them and have identified a couple of candidates who can make way, including changes required before then, to free up enough budget to fund the upgrade. Two Gameweeks down the line, Alexander-Arnold gets injured. It's time to revisit the plan. You can't have

Trent any more, but the fact that Liverpool have good fixtures hasn't changed. Who will be filling in for Trent at right back? Would you be willing to bring in another Liverpool defender instead? If so, the replacement is likely to be cheaper. Perhaps this is a good thing. Maybe the imminent sacrifice required to bring in Trent no longer needs to be made in order to fund the move? Suddenly, you may find you have enough budget to improve your squad in the short term. This could lead to a whole new branch of possibilities, while still keeping the original plan contextually relevant.

A very successful businessman once said to me, "If you don't know where you are going, then how are you going to get there?"

Forward planning does not mean sticking rigidly to a set plan. It means setting out a vision for the future of your squad based on the best information available at the time. When that information changes, the plan must alter accordingly. But to do this, you need to have a plan in the first place.

2. BE HUMBLE, HONEST AND OBJECTIVE ABOUT YOUR FPL PERFORMANCE

At the beginning of this chapter, I took the opportunity to do some self-reflection. In many ways, writing this book has forced me to do this. We all have our own ways of absorbing information optimally; mine is through the written word. Whichever way works best for you, taking the time to review your season, and to reflect on the good and the bad, is an essential step in improving in future seasons. This is a shared trait amongst the Elite XI managers.

As I mentioned earlier in the book, one of the things which struck me about the members of the Elite XI was how humble they were about their FPL prowess. This is not a gift they simply take for granted, but a skill they have earned through hard work, dedication and self-reflection.

When I surveyed the group, every single Elite XI member said that they were receptive to feedback from others, even if that feedback was negative. Of those, 75% said that reflecting on and objectively evaluating FPL decisions was either 'somewhat or very' important. Two-thirds said they were happy to admit to – and correct – previous errors, and just over half of the respondents said they put aside time at the end of the season to do a full review of where things went wrong, with a view to improving in the subsequent season.

3. SEEK INFORMATION FROM HIGH-QUALITY SOURCES

The amount of information available to FPL managers is staggering. Beyond the old-school option – watching all the matches, which alone would require roughly 20 hours of your time every single week – there is now a great plethora of footballing statistics for us to digest. As we know, this data goes beyond goals and assists and right down into expected data and underlying statistics.

On top of this, there is a burgeoning FPL community full of content creators (small and large), expressing their opinions daily. There are innumerable podcasts, YouTube channels, TikToks, Spaces meetings on X, not to mention the surge in information now available on the Fantasy Premier League official website courtesy of The Scout and other prominent voices from the FPL community.

As the saying goes, 'knowledge is power', and this is certainly true for our Elite XI members. All of those surveyed said that the information they use to support their FPL decisions comes from a wide variety of sources. The more information they can get their hands on, the better.

When I surveyed the group about their information preferences, the breadth of information sources was quite amazing. Of the multiple sources of info available, most (92%) regarded Premier League press conferences and trusted sources of team leaks as important information.

A close second (at 83%) was statistics. This was level with watching the matches live and/or watching match highlights. This corroborates my belief that a combination of both statistical analysis and eye test is the best combination for making FPL decisions.

Three-quarters of our Elite XI managers get their information from dedicated FPL websites such as Fantasy Football Fix. The great advantage of this medium of information is that FPL websites are a one-stop shop for everything managers need to make their decisions. Fixture planners, AI prediction models, stats areas and manager team reveals are amongst the top features and tools sought out on websites.

Podcasts are used by two-thirds of our managers and a little over half get their information from both AI prediction tools and discussing FPL with like-minded friends and/or colleagues.

It is impossible to absorb all the information available on the internet and, even if you could, a lot of it is contradictory. Hosts and guests of podcasts will invariably arrive at different conclusions, as will friends and colleagues. As we have seen earlier in Part Two, statistics are only as useful as how they are interpreted and there can be great variance in how this is done. Even a brief sojourn on FPL Twitter will leave your head spinning. If you go on there seeking an answer, you may find yourself coming away with five more questions. So, what then should we do with all this information?

Deciding this is in itself a skill. The first part is to utterly reject information from sources you do not trust. If you make a last-minute transfer based on leaked team news from a fake source, the result could be disastrous. Likewise, if you take advice from – or are swayed by – someone whose playing style differs from your own, then you could end up making decisions incompatible with your squad set-up.

The key is to carefully curate your sources of trusted information and filter everything else out. Mark Mansfield favours FPL Blackbox over the other podcasts. His reason for this is that they provide the full picture, particularly when presenting statistics. Mark feels instinctively that they are not pushing a narrative but objectively analysing the evidence, looking at both sides of the coin. This does not mean that FPL Blackbox is better than other podcasts out there, it simply means that it gives the Mark the information he feels he needs to aid his decisions.

This does not mean that you should isolate yourself from all new or foreign information sources, but if you do start to absorb FPL content from fresh sources, approach them with a level of scepticism until they prove themselves both trustworthy and compatible with your playing style.

4. PRIORITISE FIXTURES OVER FORM

In my previous book, I explored the fixtures over form debate. When it comes down to it, what is more important: a player's form, or the fixtures ahead of him?[20]

My conclusion is that it is usually possible to find both, but if I had to choose one, it would be fixtures. I am a very fixture-driven player (often to my detriment). But it is heartening to know that this strategy is shared by 100% of the Elite XI group.

When every Elite XI manager is in agreement with something, it means that something is worth paying attention to.

One of the things I notice amongst newer, or more casual, FPL managers is that they have a tendency to 'chase last week's points'. Writing articles for Fix means that I spend a lot of time doing player ownership analysis; I can confirm that goals scored (rather than underlying data) is by far the biggest driver of transfer activity.

There is an argument to say that a Premier League footballer's good showing in a single match can

---

[20] For the sake of clarity, 'form' in this context is described as returns in the form of FPL points. When we talk about form in this regard, we essentially mean attacking returns, bonus points, clean sheets etc. rather than underlying data – shots, xG, xA etc.

breed further good performance down the line. There is some merit to this argument. Confidence plays a significant role in a player's performance. There is nothing like scoring a goal to give a player a lift both in that game and in the next one.

But, unfortunately, this works both ways, and going into a game full of confidence is no guarantee of an attacking return. If the attacking return doesn't come, then a drop in confidence could ensue. Confidence is a near-impossible thing to assess, and even if we could it is not just past returns which contribute to it. Personal circumstances, something a teammate said to them in the changing rooms, a disparaging look from the coach during a training session. These are things which cannot be quantified or assessed. Not to mention the fact that some players are motivated by the desire to turn their poor performances around.

Fixtures, on the other hand, are a more reliable predictor of future returns. Assuming a standard level of confidence from all players, the most logical assumption that we can make is that any given player is more likely to score against a team with a weaker defence than it is against a team with a strong defence. For our reliable goal scorers and premium attackers, we increase major haul potential against weaker teams and therefore should consider a route to owning the best possible captaincy options for a given period, based on upcoming fixtures.

According to our Elite XI managers, the best possible combination is to merge fixtures with underlying data. That is to say, target the players who have the best fixtures and the best underlying data. If a player is constantly racking up high xG and shot volume, and is about to enter a period in the schedule where his team plays weaker opposition, then this is a recipe for upcoming returns. Even better if the player hasn't recently scored, as the 'poor form' will mean potential suitors will not be attracted to them, which will keep their price from going up and their ownership low.

5. DON'T WORRY ABOUT EFFECTIVE OWNERSHIP, BUT DON'T IGNORE IT EITHER

Effective Ownership is one of the aspects of Fantasy Premier League that can be quite difficult to describe to someone who is not highly engaged with the game. In the same way that it can feel long-winded and cumbersome to explain the importance of expected data to someone who has zero interest in football analytics, it is also tricky to explain the importance of EO to a casual player. Believe me, I've tried.

The best way to describe the importance of EO to the uninitiated is to ask if they have ever had a really good Gameweek in terms of their points total, but have lost overall rank. People often forget the simple fact that success in FPL is about how we perform relative to others, not in isolation. This is where EO can guide us, but it is not straightforward.

For example, if Player A is 60% owned and scores a hat-trick, then it is reasonable to assume that not owning him is going to be damaging. But, for all we know, a large proportion of that 60% could be from a rank tier which is so far away that the impact won't be felt. Generally speaking, ownership of a popular player tends to be distributed throughout the ranks, but there are occasions where it gets skewed. Imagine, for example, Mo Salah, who is highly owned at the beginning of a season (as he generally is).

Imagine now that he picks up a long-term injury or goes to AFCON. Engaged managers will probably free up that budget and make a plan to bring Salah back at a later date. However, this may not be reflected in the overall ownership statistics.

Most of the teams which sink to the bottom of the overall rankings are ghost teams from FPL managers who have long since given up. Most of them are likely to own Salah simply because they are no longer managing their squads. They will inadvertently become the beneficiaries of his return to action, but those managers occupy a rank tier which needn't trouble engaged players.

The trick, therefore, is to check ownership relative to your own rank tier. This will give you a much better idea of how owned a player is by FPL managers who you are competing with. In other words, it will let you know how damaging – or otherwise – a player will be in real terms. One of my favourite Fix tools, Insight Live, tells you everything you need to know about player EO. Other tools – such as Fix Rivals and Rank Prediction – help you keep an eye on your mini-league rivals and allow you to play with potential scenarios to see how they will affect your overall rank.

This all being said, becoming overly obsessed with EO can lead to managers making the wrong decisions at the wrong time. A player's EO should never override what you think is the best overall decision. When our Elite XI managers say that they don't worry about Effective Ownership but they keep an eye on it, here's what they mean by way of example.

First off, if you have identified Player X as being the best player to bring in for your stated time period, then whether he is owned by 50% of players in your rank tier or by 1%, he is the player you should go for. No questions.

But, as we know, there is usually more than one candidate vying for our attention, and no matter to what degree we drill down into the available data, there is usually at least a 50/50 decision to be made. More often than not, this actually boils down to a choice of a few candidates, not just two. This is where we can factor EO into our decision-making process.

But first we need to get a feel for where we currently are versus our objectives. This is quite difficult at the beginning of the season when the rank tiers are compressed. Small variances in points can lead to dramatic jumps/falls in rank, so early on I tend to err on the side of caution. But as the season progresses, we can get a better feel of how we are doing.

Let's say it is towards the end of the season and my transfer decision is between Player A (owned by 30% of managers in my rank tier) and Player B (owned by

5% of managers in my rank tier). The first thing I need to ask myself is, where am I relative to where I want to be? My target is usually to finish in the Top 100k. With the number of registered FPL squads out there, this, to me, has always been a very respectable target (more on this later.)

If I am ranked around 100k, I would probably lean toward wishing to protect my rank, and the best way to do this is to match the moves of the managers around me, in which case I would go for Player A. If it goes wrong, so be it, an opportunity was missed but the overall damage is negligible.

If I am ranked at 500k, then I have a lot of work to do to make up the difference between where I am and where I want to be, and not much time in which to do it. If there is an opportunity to punt on a low-owned player, then I need to take it. If I get it right, I can reduce the gap more quickly (by bringing in Player B). Of course, the great risk is that the wrong decision is made, which could contribute to a rank drop, making the gap even wider. This is a vicious cycle low-ranked managers can fall into, but it is also the risk which must be taken.

6. ANALYSE STATISTICS (BUT THE RIGHT ONES)

This, to a degree, is covered by Part Two of this book – particularly with the Corey and James case study – but it cannot be ignored that most of our Elite XI cohort regularly analyse FPL statistics and that they play a big part in their FPL decisions.

The problem with statistics is that there are a plethora of metrics to consider, and each can be interpreted in different ways. I do not profess to be an expert in statistical analysis when it comes to FPL; in fact, using them is usually a secondary consideration for me. This passage therefore is not geared towards me telling you how to do it, but to observing how our Elite XI managers tend to approach their practical application.

First off, which stats should we pay the most attention to?

Over three-quarters of the Elite XI group selected Non-Penalty Expected Goals (NPxG) as one of their three most important metrics, while Expected Assists (xA) was selected by two-thirds.

Corey and James both prioritise xG and xA Per 90 minutes as their favoured metrics. Corey cheats a little here and uses a compound metric which can be expressed as: Non-Penalty Expected Goal Involvements Per 90 Minutes (NPxGI/90). In simple terms, this is the amount of xG (excluding penalties) and xA which a player accumulates, on average, per 90 minutes of football.

This is a powerful compound metric, because it does a number of things at once.

First, it looks at Expected Goals (xG) which, if we are looking at singular (rather than compound) metrics, is probably the most important. Expected data is not perfect, but it is by far the best metric we have access to as it looks at the quality of chances, rather than actual output. Regularly receiving high-quality chances is a better indicator of future potential than the number of goals already scored. The former is indicative of a player's ability to get into good positions, even if goal conversion didn't occur. Whereas the latter shows us outcomes irrespective of unsustainable fluke (if a player's low xG shot takes a deflection and goes in, we record and celebrate the goal and make decisions based on it).

Second, it removes penalties from the equation. Depending on which stat provider you look at, taking a spot kick gives the penalty taker an xG of 0.76 (roughly 76% of penalties are scored). This causes a large discrepancy when it comes to the utility of xG. We use xG to identify which players are getting into good positions and generating high-quality chances (or at least numerous low-to-mid-quality chances). But if a player gets 0.76 xG added to their match total for simply being the nominated penalty taker, then this warps the picture we are trying to paint. Of course, a player being the nominated penalty taker is an important consideration. However, for purposes of proper statistical analysis, it is 'cleaner' if we remove it from the xG picture.

Third, it includes, rather than omits, xA. Assists, while secondary to goals in terms of FPL points, are still a vital source of point accumulation in FPL. By including them in the calculation, it saves us having to look at a different metric.

Finally, and perhaps most importantly, the metric is expressed as an average of time spent on the pitch. If Player A has played 90 minutes of every game in a season, you would expect his xG total to be higher than that of Player B, who has been injured for four months. For all we know, Player B's xG – proportional to their time on the pitch – could be higher, making them the more potent player of the two. Assuming both players are now fit, we need to know the data per 90 minutes, rather than the totals, which will be skewed due to the variance in player minutes.

Organising all the players by this metric is a powerful way of showing who have been the top-performing players in a season. In most cases, the goal and assist output in real terms will not be too far away from the expected data. But sometimes it can help us identify those who have been over-performing (and are likely to stop doing so) and those who have been under-performing (and will soon start bagging points).

Shot volume

But there is another metric which the Elite XI find important, one I have to confess I have largely neglected, and that is 'shots'.

Corey explained to me that the reason it is important to view shots in parallel to xG is because it fine tunes the thought process as to a player's future potential. Highlighting one of the flaws of xG, Corey explains that you may have a player who, over the last four Gameweeks, has racked up an impressive xG, but this may be from one or two really golden opportunities in an otherwise barren patch. This could lead FPL managers to bring in a player whose attacking potential is quite low but has been inflated by a one-off event.

A crafty way around this is to also look at that player's shot volume for the same period. If the player has an xG of, say, 1.5 but has taken just two shots in the same period, then we can assume that the player has had two very good opportunities but otherwise hasn't been shooting.

Likewise, if a player has an xG of 1.5 but has taken six shots, then we can be assured that the player is going for goal on a more regular basis and perhaps be more confident in a recurrence of this going forwards.

This works both ways, of course. If a player has an xG of 1.5 but has taken 15 shots in that period, then this is indicative of a high number of low-quality opportunities. If you've taken 15 shots and only accumulated an xG of 1.5, then you are probably taking pot shots from 35 yards out when perhaps passing to a teammate was the better option. This, therefore, may be an FPL asset to avoid.

Time period to consider

Earlier in the book, we highlighted the dilemma which arises from deciding the time period of data that we should evaluate. More data is better, so not going back far enough could mean that we don't have a big enough sample of information and, hence, big discrepancies cannot be ironed out. Go too far back, however, and data can be skewed by big events (managerial or tactical changes etc.).

I asked the Elite XI team how far they go back when reviewing stats and found that the sweet spot seems to be between 6 and 8 Gameweeks, with 55% of respondents focusing on this time frame. A third of the Elite XI managers look at the entire season's data, and the remaining 11% look back between 9 and 10 Gameweeks. Interestingly, none of our managers look at a horizon which is five Gameweeks or less.

A good rule of thumb, therefore, is to look back six Gameweeks when analysing statistics, and look ahead six Gameweeks when considering upcoming fixtures. That keeps you with enough data to make reliable predictions, while not examining a time period so large that some of the information may have become irrelevant.[21]

---

[21] Unless of course, like James, you are able to apply footballing context to your review of statistics and manually iron out any anomalies. In which case, reviewing a larger period of data will give a more accurate picture.

7. LEAVE YOUR EGO AT THE DOOR

I'll be honest, I did not ask the Elite XI managers, "Hey guys, do you have big egos?" As a result, this recommendation is subjective rather than measurable. But I write this with a high degree of confidence, having worked with these people for years.

Ego – or FPL persona, maintaining appearances etc. – can be a real problem for FPL managers, especially those who have an online social media presence dedicated to the game.

If you regularly post to social media about your FPL team, you (inadvertently[22]) build up a persona or FPL alter ego. Over time, people will start to identify you as having a certain playing style. For some people, this is a by-product of their interactions. For others, it is something they deliberately inflate for purposes of engagement, or for reasons only known to them. We all know someone from FPL circles who fancies themselves as a bit of a renegade, or who prides themselves as someone who goes against the grain, always putting the armband on a differential option.

The trouble is, once you gain a reputation for a certain thing, it can be quite difficult to peel yourself away from that line of thinking. Whether consciously

---

[22] Or, perhaps, intentionally.

or not, your decision-making will start to align with your persona, even if it is not the optimal thing to do at that time. Someone who is known to be a bit of a maverick may struggle to captain an in-form Salah who is playing Luton, because there is an expectation that they will go against the obvious pick.

Conversely, the same weight of expectation may hamper those who pride themselves on playing the game in a risk-averse way. Where a patient and sensible manager may feel emboldened to take an off-the-wall punt because she gets a gut feeling about a player, such a manager who regularly posts content online may be worried about looking foolish, should their punt not come off.

FPL Twitter is generally a very nice community, and most people would rather see you lifted up than down in the gutter. Unfortunately, in the wild west of online social interactions, you inevitably get people who like to kick a person when they are down, or hindsight merchants who get a buzz from pointing out how foolish your decision was. Sadly, it tends to be these comments which stick in the memory. If you play the game a certain way – and play it consistently this way – you get to at least partially deflect any criticism for a bad move. If you go against your usual playing style and it backfires, you feel like an idiot. And feeling like an idiot in a very public forum is not a pleasant experience.

The problem with this fear is that it fosters a non-flexible way of playing. Sometimes, the patient manager should be bold and listen to their gut. And sometimes the thrill-seeking, differential-loving FPL manager should just do the right thing and captain the obvious choice. Sometimes we can make (or fail to make) a lot of decisions for the wrong reasons. And often, we don't even realise we are doing it.

One thing which was very clear to me from the start was the fact that our Elite XI managers didn't seem to have such hang-ups about their decision-making. This is, in part, because they are not particularly active on social media. In fact, just 17% say that they 'post often' about FPL. Amongst the others, a third say that they only post 'occasionally' and the rest either don't have an account at all or they use social media for seeking information rather than sharing it.

Fábio Borges is often praised as being one of the best (if not *the* best) FPL managers of all time.[23] He has no social media presence whatsoever and would probably be shocked to discover just how much of an icon he is in the FPL community. Some of his transfer decisions seem downright crazy; fortunately

---

[23] Fábio's worst ever finish was 33k in the 2022/23 season. Between 2015 and 2022, he earned seven back-to-back Top 5k finishes – amongst those were finishes of 95, 222 and 671.

for him, he doesn't have to justify them to anyone. He just happily trundles along with one of the best FPL careers anyone has ever seen.

So, how exactly do you stop external opinion influencing your FPL moves? The simplest way, as mentioned earlier, is to delete your FPL-specific social media or, at the very least, stop sharing your transfers, captaincy decisions or current rank. This, however, may be a step too far for some people who enjoy being part of the FPL community. Indeed, being an active member of the FPL community does come with benefits, such as up-to-date news at our fingertips, refined and filtered data, and opinions from some of the best FPL around. It also connects you with fans of other clubs, allowing you to fill in knowledge gaps. I certainly don't know who the preferred back-up player in each position is for every club. But I can find somebody in the community who supports the team in question very quickly indeed.

The first thing you need to do is have an honest conversation with yourself. Cards on the table, has your FPL decision-making been influenced by concern for what others will think or say? If so, has the net result been that you have missed opportunities or been forced into making mistakes you wouldn't ordinarily have made?[24] If the answer

---

[24] Let's not forget, fear of what others may think/say could, on balance, have done you a favour!

to the above two questions is yes, then you have identified a problem which needs resolving.

Perhaps there is a middle ground. Why not consider a different approach to the content you distribute on social media? You don't have to share your squad screenshots, weekly scores or overall rank. But you can still use it to share your opinions. You can still use it to obtain valuable information. If people don't know what moves you are making, they cannot criticise you for them. With this comes a certain power. A lot of FPL success involves spotting opportunities others haven't, and/or knowing when to go against the consensus (see Mark Mansfield in Part Two). You may feel freer to make these bold calls if your squad isn't under the microscope of public opinion.

PART FOUR

ELITE PSYCHOLOGY

Early on in the 2022/23 campaign, I had a (quasi-self-inflicted) captaincy mishap which ruined the rest of the season for me. Things had started pretty well. I was ranked 199k in Gameweek 5, which was a solid start. By Gameweek 8, I had slipped slightly, to 227k, which was no big deal. I had planned to play my Wildcard in Gameweek 9 to take advantage of the fixture swings, but it was turning out to be trickier than I had anticipated.

Manchester City and Arsenal – the in-form teams – both had a confirmed blank in Gameweek 12. Liverpool were suffering from poor form and, like Arsenal and Spurs, they had tricky fixtures on the horizon. It made it difficult to come up with a definitive strategy. Looking ahead, I decided to sacrifice some short-term gains to set up my squad for the foreseeable future. Gameweek 9 was one I wished to simply get out of the way, but I was optimistic about how things would pan out thereafter.

Captaincy was a difficult decision in this Gameweek. Leicester had a home game against Nottingham Forest, and my instinct was telling me to put the armband on James Maddison, which is where I left it all week. As I got nearer to the deadline, the little voices in my head were telling me that perhaps I should consider changing the captaincy to Erling Haaland. City had a home game against Manchester

United which, while not the best fixture, was probably the safest option due to the fact that the masses were captaining the Norwegian and, as we know, he has proven himself to have a very high ceiling. So, as FPL managers do, I started tinkering.

Another aspect of my Wildcard dilemma was whether to bring in Mohamed Salah or Kevin De Bruyne. After much back-and-forth, I decided to go with the Belgian. Liverpool were still to prove themselves this season whereas City already looked to be firing on all cylinders.

Sometimes (I don't know if I am alone in this) I like to move the armband around, just to see how it feels on certain players. That may sound weird, but it usually triggers some thought processes in my head. On deadline day I moved the captaincy to Kevin De Bruyne, but instantly felt I couldn't connect with the decision; I knew right away that I would either put it back on Maddison or play safe and go with Haaland. In the end, I submitted to my risk-averse nature and decided to put it on Haaland. No point going against the grain this early on in the season.

I moved the captaincy to Haaland and took a screenshot.[25] I also left the vice captaincy on

---

[25] Back in those days I used to document all my moves on both Instagram and Twitter and would post my team and reasoning pre-deadline.

Maddison, because I still had a gut feeling he was going to return big and if Haaland ended up injured or the City game was postponed, Maddison made more sense than De Bruyne as vice.

When I hit 'Save My Team' there was an error and the website crashed. I actually remember seeing the line 'You are not authorised to make these changes' amongst jumbled-up code and characters. It was not something I had ever experienced on the website.

My heart sank because, around this time, there was a huge scandal involving one of the other fantasy football websites. Unhappy at their employer's alleged lackadaisical approach to online security, a disgruntled former employee hacked into their system and exported a ton of user data, including email addresses, passwords and bank account details. The hacker then posted all this information publicly to highlight the poor security they were so aggrieved about. As a former subscriber to this website, my own details had been compromised.

Shortly after this happened, several people in the FPL community had their accounts hijacked; in many cases the hackers gained access to their squads and made lots of changes, including season-ending numbers of points hits for injured players and the like.

In the aftermath of the hacking scandal I had, of course, immediately changed all my passwords and cancelled the bank card in question. I had assumed all was well, but seeing the message about 'not having the authority' to make changes made me think that perhaps someone had hacked in and changed my password while I was playing with my squad.

This was hours before the actual deadline, so I ruled out the FPL server being at capacity. I logged back in and got access straight away with no issues. Suitably spooked – but incredibly relieved – I changed my password again (perhaps unnecessarily) and checked over my team. No changes had been made – although, as I was on Wildcard, there were no changes which couldn't have been easily undone – my bench and captaincy were as I had left them. All was well.

Fast forward to Sunday 2nd October 2022 and I was lying on the couch in the lounge, following the football on the live text. My wife was sewing up a rip in our son's ever-damaged jeans, and both our children were playing nicely together. As a parent of young children, you learn to savour these moments of quiet while they last. Precious like a bubble which you know can burst at any time.

It was the second half at the Etihad. The Manchester derby was not going well for the red half of the city.

Manchester City were 4-0 up, Foden and Haaland with a brace apiece. Both of Haaland's goals had been assisted by De Bruyne so my decision to go for KDB over Salah on my Wildcard was looking good so far.

Soon after, Anthony Martial earned United a consolation goal, but in the 64th minute, Haaland would bag his hat-trick.[26] I remember thinking to myself how glad I was that I had changed my mind at the last minute and played safe with the Haaland captaincy. I felt a pang of sorrow for those who had gone against him, as I nearly had.

At this point, smugly sat on the sofa and informing my uninterested wife of my Wildcard success, I realised that I hadn't checked who my FPL nemesis (Dan) had given the armband to. I logged into FPL to find out, and my heart sank for the second time that weekend. Staring back at me was my team, but with De Bruyne – not Haaland – as captain. Determined there must have been some mistake, I refreshed, logged out, logged back in, but that captaincy symbol, like a dagger in my heart, was still on the Belgian.

Haaland (with captaincy) would have earned 46 points, as opposed to the 16 I got for De Bruyne.

---

[26] Foden would complete his own hat-trick nine minutes later.

While his two assists certainly took the edge off what would have been a complete disaster, the difference in points was significant.[27] At this stage of the season, the gap between the rank tiers was small, so this 15-point loss was significant. To add insult to injury, Maddison bagged two goals and an 18-pointer against Forest in Leicester's assured 4-0 win.

I have played FPL for 19 years. I have enjoyed huge highs and difficult lows over an FPL career spanning almost two decades. I have learned how to deal with a variety of situations. I have toughened myself against bad Gameweeks, Covid postponements, player injuries, captaincy blanks, chip failures and all the other horrible stuff FPL throws our way. But something about this was different.

Despite getting 82 points, I suffered a 21k red arrow down to a rank of 248k. But it wasn't the red arrow which bothered me, it was the manner in which it happened. In some ways, I think it would have been easier to cope with if I had just missed the deadline or totally cocked up. Don't get me wrong, I'd have still been furious, but I'd have had a word with myself and moved on. But this felt, just, well, unfair.

---

[27] People sometimes get confused with points lost/gained when it comes to captaincy decisions between two players owned by the same manager, so allow me to clarify: because I owned both players the difference in points was not 46 − 16 = 30 but 23 − 8 = 15.

I had chosen Haaland; I had physically made the change and hit save and gone about my weekend, decision made. I've never experienced that website issue before, or since, so I am not entirely sure what happened. My best guess is that while the system knew I was on Haaland prior to the crash, it hadn't registered that my last command was to save and confirm my selection and therefore defaulted to my previous selection, which was De Bruyne. I'm guessing the Pick Team screen, when finally reinstated, showed Haaland but still required me to hit Save My Team again – the crash having happened at this point. At least some portion of the blame has to be placed at my feet for not checking that the changes had been saved since the crash, but it felt like I had done everything correctly.

That 15-points-that-should-have-been haunted me for months after. Have you ever done something really embarrassing and then, months later, having not thought about it once, your mind just suddenly whacks your consciousness with a sharp reminder of the incident and makes you go 'ugh!'? It was like that.

I always say that the 2022/23 season was my least favourite in living memory. There were many aspects to this. Firstly, the way the opening fixtures fell meant that pretty much everyone seemed to have the same Gameweek 1 squad; there was very little variety to the template, and it felt like everyone was being funnelled down the same avenue in terms of transfers. To add to this, many desirable players were under-priced, which meant little compromise had to be made by managers, which (perhaps counter-intuitively) further restricted the variety.

Second, I was now writing weekly articles for Fix. This is a dream job and I wouldn't give it up for the world, but it did come with a major downside. My usual coping mechanism for disappointment (48 hours away from FPL and social media) was no longer available. It did not matter whether I had a great Gameweek or an absolute stinker; I had to muster the enthusiasm to write an article about all those big-hitting, highly owned players who weren't in my squad. This was surprisingly difficult to adapt to.

Another significant factor was the fact that a few people in my life had either died, come close to dying or discovered they had a terminal illness. This really shone a light on how precious time was. It made me re-assess how I spent my time and, after a sort of personal 'audit', I concluded I was allocating too much time to social media. This led to me withdrawing a bit from the online FPL community.

The reason I share this anecdote is that it highlights that even a veteran of the game such as myself – with all the battle scars a long FPL career will give you – can still encounter something which can have a dramatic impact on the joy of the game. Sometimes the blip is temporary, and all it takes is a big green arrow to set you right. But sometimes it is longer lasting and even a healthy rank boost isn't enough to rekindle your love for FPL.

The same is true of the Elite XI. In some ways, they are under even more pressure to do well, their reputation being contingent on consistently good finishes. It is therefore pertinent to try to unlock the secrets of a positive mindset. How do the very best managers cope with the pressure? Do they use special coping mechanisms to deal with a terrible Gameweek? What sort of 'comeback' can we realistically expect to have if the first half of our season has fallen to pieces?

This part deals with the psychological aspects of FPL, in particular how to cope when things go wrong.

ELITE PSYCHOLOGY

Naturally, to find out how to cultivate an elite mindset, I needed to speak to one of the Elite XI managers, and I was particularly interested in speaking to Andrew Neave. This was for two reasons.

First, Andrew has only recently created a dedicated FPL Twitter account. It was from here that he was identified by Fix, eventually leading him (along with Tim Walpole) to become one of the newest members of the Elite XI squad. This is obviously a huge transition for someone to take. Going from someone who sits quietly in the background, answering to no one, and making whichever decisions they deem necessary, to suddenly being thrust into the public eye with the expectations that come with a label such as 'elite manager'.

Second, he had a shocking first half to the season and was ranked at 1.4m in Gameweek 15. This was a first for Andrew, who had never before had such a poor start. Andrew managed to turn this around and is, at the time of writing in Gameweek 32, ranked 74k, with his Bench Boost still left to play.

I wanted to see if there was any correlation between the pressure of joining the Elite XI team – as well as the creation of an online FPL persona – and his poor start. More importantly, I wanted to know what he did to overcome this bad start and put himself on course for a great finish.

Background

Andrew works as a freelance creative resource manager and has lived in London for the last ten years. Before that he lived in South Africa, his home country, where he was introduced to FPL in the 2011/12 season by his group of friends. Like Ireland, South Africa is another non-UK country where the Premier League is a really big deal. Andrew is still in touch with his friends from back home, and FPL rivalry is at the core of their friendship.

"I've been in the same mini-league with my mates for 13 years now. Whenever we get in touch, FPL is the common denominator. It's usually the first thing we talk about."

In terms of playing style, Andrew definitely falls more under the eye test camp rather than stats. Andrew describes himself as a straightforward and safe kind of manager, foregoing bold moves in favour of making the correct decision. He is happy to take hits, but only when fixtures and form converge for a long-term pick. Not the biggest user of stats, Andrew uses his own intuition and footballing knowledge to guide his decisions.

"I like to keep it simple and take a fairly safe approach for most of the season. When looking at transfers, if it seems like the most obvious move – even if it's a boring one – it's probably the right move. I prefer fixtures over form, as I believe fixtures bring form. I'm not really a stats man, but I do enjoy doing a bit of research and seeing if the stats back up my thinking. I set up my squad with certain 'price points' to make it easy to move for in-form players and adapt to any surprise performers. I do chase price rises at the very start of the season, but only if I know I want that player regardless."

This direct approach to FPL has paid dividends. Andrew bagged a Top 10k finish in his debut season. Since then, he has racked up 5 x Top 5k finishes, and 7 x Top 10k finishes. His best season was in 2015/16, when he finished 589th globally.

Last season, he finished painfully close to getting his second Top 1k finish, with a final rank of 1,022 and, in the summer break, he was snapped up by Fix and made an official member of the Elite XI. The transition has been difficult for Andrew, who now realises how delicately balanced the thought processes which have brought him so much FPL success were, and how easily they can be disrupted.

"Before [Fix] I had a personal Twitter account which I used to gather FPL information, but I never posted my own team, so I was relatively anonymous in that regard. Then, when I started sharing my weekly scores on a new dedicated FPL account – and then joined Fix – that's when my mentality started to change."

I asked Andrew if he thought there was any correlation between a more overt online presence and his worst ever start to FPL.

"Oh yeah, definitely. The first time I noticed I was playing differently was when I realised that I was reluctant to steer too far away from my Manager's Notes.[28] I also realised that I was trying to take on too much information. I've always been fairly confident in my own ability, but all of a sudden, I am surrounded by all these managers who have ranks as good as mine, and some even better. So, I was being swayed by their opinions even though their playing styles are totally different from mine."

Andrew played his Wildcard in Gameweek 5, but progress up the ranks was slow. A combination of bad luck – including a savage string of injuries (see Part One of the book) – and an unexpected change in Andrew's playing style meant that his ability to catch up quickly was stunted.

---

[28] Manager's Notes are a feature of the Elite XI: Team Reveal tool, a space where the Elite XI managers jot down their current thoughts for the next Gameweek, enabling members to get real-time insights into each individual's strategy and future plans.

But, all of a sudden, around Gameweek 16, he began to shoot through the ranks. I asked Andrew what changed.

"I just took a good, hard look at myself. I knew I'd had bad luck with injuries, but it was more than that. I had to be honest with myself and find out where I was letting myself down. That's when I realised I was not playing FPL my way any more. I was trying to consider too much information, but it wasn't all the right information. I felt like I had to deep dive into stats, which isn't my thing, and I was being talked out of moves by what other people were saying."

To put things right, Andrew decided it was time to return to the basics. He started with a big cull on social media. He went through his followers, line by line, and removed any who didn't correlate with his own playing style. He started listening to his own gut more, reverting to the eye test to inform his decisions and using stats only as a litmus test rather than the main steer.

The effects of these changes were dramatic. Between Gameweek 15 and 21, he rose from 1.4m to 537k. Six back-to-back green arrows then saw him reach 95k in Gameweek 27. Andrew hit a stumbling block between Gameweeks 28 and 30, but his rank stayed fairly static. He is now ranked 75k with seven Gameweeks left to play.

Mesmerised by Andrew's account of his season, I realise what a laid-back person he is. His South African accent frames a soft but clear voice, which radiates calm. It's hard to believe that this guy could ever be upset or angry at an online football game, despite the fact that I know better.

I ask him what he does to cope with the frustration of a bad Gameweek.

"If I have a bad Gameweek, I just totally switch off from football and FPL. I don't watch *Match of the Day*, I don't go on Twitter. I just have a break from it until I am ready to come back. I have no interest in watching the player who has destroyed my rank, nor do I want to see everyone posting their great scores."

I rounded off the interview by asking Andrew to imagine he was about to meet someone who was having a bad season and was perhaps thinking about changing their approach to FPL, or even quitting it altogether. What one piece of advice would he give them?

"One or two Gameweeks don't define a season. Don't lose sight of the bigger picture, and keep on doing what you feel is right. Many FPL managers feel like they have to adapt their ways to catch up, but most of the time this actually makes things worse. You don't have to make the off-the-wall transfer, or captain differentials. Don't be afraid of making the boring choice, so long as it is the right one."

Andrew's closing comments lead us nicely into another important piece of advice when it comes to having a bad FPL season: no matter how bleak things look, don't give up!

NEVER GIVE UP!

If, having heard Andrew's comeback story, you are still not convinced as to the scale of what is possible midway through an FPL season, then I'd like to introduce you to Craig (otherwise known as FPL Editor) and his miraculous comeback in the 2022/23 season.

Craig is a freelance sports writer. I met him through the FPL community, but actually ended up working with him later on. Like me, he writes weekly FPL articles for Fix.

Craig is not a member of the Elite XI, but boasts an impressive FPL record nonetheless. With 5 x Top 10k finishes, which include 2 x Top 5k finishes, Craig has played FPL since his debut season in 2010. Excluding his first season, in which he joined halfway through, Craig's worst rank was 177k in the 2016/17 season. This happened to coincide with the birth of his first child, so Craig can be forgiven for lacking his usual focus.

This section of the book is not to celebrate Craig's FPL career, however, but to illustrate the sort of turnaround which is possible with more than half of the season already gone. In the 2022/23 season, Craig had his worst ever start. In Gameweek 21 he was ranked just outside the 1m mark. One excellent result in Gameweek 22 saw him bag 107 points, halving his overall rank to 515k. Being ranked 1m and 500k are very different positions to be in. To be able to move from one to another in just a single Gameweek illustrates how quickly your FPL perspectives can shift.

From here, Craig went on an absolute points spree! Back-to-back green arrows culminated in a Top 6k finish by the end of the season. To truly appreciate the immensity of this comeback, I have presented Craig's overall rank by Gameweek in the table below:

Gameweek	Overall Rank
38	5,988
37	10,087
36	12,625
35	31,797
34	33,668
33	55,286
32	88,516
31	105,187
30	142,903
29	161,784
28	308,761
27	338,834
26	436,313
25	644,711
24	521,829
23	559,270
22	515,937
21	1,059,845

I decided I needed to talk to Craig about this immense comeback. As I saw it, there were only three options which could explain it.

1. His season was going terribly, so he changed tactics halfway through the season. (If this was the case, I wanted to know what he changed.)

2. He had started the season with a different approach and decided to go back to his normal playing style (in which case I wanted to know what he did differently in the beginning and what his normal playing style is).

3. Or he didn't change anything at all and the tides of fortune simply turned in his favour.

Craig, like me, has struggled with a challenging season in 2023/24. He opens the conversation by reflecting just how quickly one can be humbled by FPL. Never were truer words spoken. His miraculous comeback season seems something of a distant memory, deeply buried under the very present torments being faced.

"In all honestly, I always just do me. I never change style, so to speak. I am quite aggressive out of the blocks, not afraid of taking hits, and will do what is required to build team value. So I suppose I do this to the detriment of my rank early on, knowing that I can build on it later. In that sense, it has probably been about five or six seasons since I had a really decent start to FPL."

Craig's style is to go aggressive in the opening Gameweeks with a big focus on building team value. He keeps his chips in his back pocket, knowing that using a Wildcard or Free Hit with an above-average team value is a powerful combination which can be deployed later on in the season.

This tactic is not uncommon but, interestingly, is one which is a divisive topic amongst the Elite XI. When asked 'Do you believe building team value is important?' 50% of the Elite XI responded that it is not. Of the half that do believe it is important, 50% said only at the beginning of the season, while the other half maintain their team value throughout the season. While I personally do not prioritise team value, I suspect there is no correct answer to this question. Doing so has certainly been working out well for Craig.

The focus, however, should not be on Craig's playing style but rather on his unwavering commitment to it. Craig has a plan and sticks to it, come hell or high water. When the season is looking grim, he doesn't change his tactics midway through. All you need sometimes is for the wheel of fortune to spin in your favour. Craig's comeback is a testament to that.

Many FPL managers, when looking at a low rank with more than half the season gone, make the fatal mistake of taking more risks (or fewer risks if your usual playing style is aggressive), or going against their own playing style in order to make up lost ground. But in most cases, simply sticking to your guns, staying committed and disciplined and trusting the process can be enough to finish on a high.

As with many parts of this book, I was secretly hoping to stumble on some magical formula which would help my readers turn things around in a bad season. But the reality is, you've just got to keep doing the next right thing, as Craig did.

Of course, you need a big dollop of luck thrown in and one cannot expect to make such a profound comeback every season.[29] But the above table shows what is possible and should serve as a strong reminder to just keep going, no matter how bad things look!

---

[29] As both Craig and I are discovering in the 2023/24 season!

CONCLUSION

When I wrote my previous book, the Conclusion was very straightforward. After starting with one of my favourite FPL anecdotes[30] I then went on to summarise the tips and tricks I had provided in the book. As I had written the book chronologically – starting with pre-season, then moving on through the Gameweeks – this was relatively easy to do; the finished product was a high-level summary detailing the roadmap of a typical FPL season.

Writing this book has been fascinating. I didn't set out with any preconceived notion of how the book would turn out, nor did I attempt to steer it in any sort of direction. A part of me really hoped that an 'elite formula' would present itself as I was putting pen to paper but, deep down, I knew this wouldn't be the case. I have no problem with this; however, it makes writing the Conclusion somewhat more difficult.

Much of what I have learned from the Elite XI while writing this book concerns FPL behaviours and strategies which are already embedded in the way I play. Other aspects which have surfaced are things I

---

[30] About the time I had to explain to Emmanuel Adebayor – in person! – why I had removed him from my FPL team.

don't plan to implement, because they don't really correlate with my playing style. For example, while I am in awe of Corey's data-scraping FPL macros, this is not something I intend to implement into my own way of playing FPL. There are, however, a number of things which have surfaced from all my research, which would work well with my playing style, and I am sure will enhance my FPL performance going forward.

In order to use this book practically, I am going to create a plan for next season. I will cast aside anything which I already do – or at least wilfully intend not to do – and focus on an improvement plan which will take me from where I am now to the next level. This conclusion therefore is a simple, five-point blueprint for raising my game next season.

Once you have read my plan (assuming you are interested in reading it), I would invite you, the reader, to make your own, based on what you have learned from reading this book.

ELITE LESSONS LEARNED

1. Evaluate the previous season objectively

Review, analyse and improve. This is something that the Elite XI managers do incredibly well, be it deliberately or subconsciously.

An example of how to do this is provided in Part Three, where, ahead of Gameweek 30, I used the international break to review the season. I knew it had gone badly, but I wanted to know why and find out if there was anything I could have done differently to improve it. I don't mean with the benefit of hindsight ("I should have captained the player who scored the most points"), but to see if there were decisions which were bad at the time, based on all available information. As it happens, there were plenty, and those are what we need to really zoom into.

Many FPL managers are content to just say, "That was a horrible season, I got unlucky" and leave it there. And, of course, there is always the chance that nothing but sheer bad luck was the culprit. Sometimes we have bad seasons, despite not making any definable errors. But, more often than not, there is something we could have done better. To stand a chance of finding out what that is, we need to ask the question first.

Quite often this is also the case when we have had a good season. One of my best in recent years (23k) was full of errors of judgement when I look back at it now. But at the time, I simply banked the good finish and moved on. Rather than taking time to say, "I may have got very lucky that year, perhaps I should improve a few things in case I don't get that good fortune again."

At the end of this season, I intend to do a full review and put together a strategy on how to improve, which will tie into the plan being outlined earlier.

2. Refine my information consumption

I think it would be fair to say that a bit of laziness crept in this season, and I leaned heavily on the information obtained by others, rather than properly gathering it myself. Using information presented by others is not necessarily a bad thing, but there is a skill to doing it, as Niklas Zanden demonstrated in Part Two. Too many times this season I have been guilty of just raising a finger into the FPL community to try to see which way the wind of opinion is blowing and then allowing myself to be swept along by it.

Fortunately, there's plenty I can do about this, and the refining of FPL information will be one of the core aspects of my plan to improve next season.

Firstly, amongst the Elite XI, I will be focusing my energy on what Mark Mansfield is doing. As I said earlier in this book, I feel that Mark's philosophy to FPL most closely aligns with mine. Corey, James and Craig are all excellent managers, but the former two are very statistics oriented, whereas Craig is much more aggressive than I am.

The weight of Mark's opinion will be much heavier next season. After all, had I listened to his advice this season, I would never have got rid of Bukayo Saka to my peril. Dan Bennett is another Elite XI manager who I will be listening to. Like me, Dan is a planner and a risk-averse/patient manager. Having both him and Mark buzzing in my ear will enable me to be exposed to differing ideas, but within the comfort zone of my own playing style.

I also plan, for the very first time, to pick a weekly podcast to listen to, and I will listen to it religiously. Which one, I do not yet know, but I shall look forward to doing some serious research. There are plenty of options out there, so it will be important for me to find one which matches my needs. While it is nice to have a good laugh, I do not need to be entertained. I also don't need a podcast which focuses on 'off the wall' picks or going against the grain. Where possible, I would like one which presents information in a complete way (not cherry-picking statistics to fit a pre-established narrative) and discusses the pros and cons of certain moves/strategies.

I will almost certainly need to change my use of Twitter next season. This will be a complicated change to implement, and the reason is twofold. First, I have made a few changes in my personal life which have put greater distance between myself and social media generally. The year 2024 has been one of 'reduction' for me. As well as a physical decluttering of my home environment, I am also decluttering the things I spend time on.

As I mentioned earlier, I have conducted a deep review and, having had an honest word with myself,

I have jotted down a long list of things which I waste my time on. Those things are being axed in favour of spending real, face-to-face time with my family and friends. Social media was top of that pile.

Thirdly, as my Twitter following grew so did the number of information sources I was exposed to. My News Feed is a mess, largely dominated by FPL accounts I know little about. Scrolling down the never-ending chasm of opinion constantly means that little bits of information gradually seep into your subconscious mind and have an impact on your decision-making. It will take time, but refining my information sources so that my News Feed only contains high-quality and trusted sources of information is an absolute priority.

Inspired by my conversation with Craig, I plan to use AI as a sense check next season. I may not know the exact weighting any given algorithm gives to the various factors which comprise their 'scoring', but there is a distinct advantage to the cold and impartial analysis AI offers. FPL is about drawing a line under the previous Gameweek and making the best decision moving forward, based on the most up-to-date information. Often, AI is better at doing this than us humans, who are often clouded by our emotions. I will not follow any algorithmic recommendation religiously, but I'll explore potential transfer combinations I had not previously considered.

3. Use statistics more efficiently

I have always preferred using my own intuition over statistics. I understand football well enough to make reasonable judgements based on what I am seeing, and I watch enough football to get a decent gist of what is happening. That being said, sometimes I am not able to catch up with highlights. And in many cases, while the viewer can trust the highlights package to hit all the major talking points of a game, they often omit critical match events from an FPL perspective. Unless singled out in the post-match analysis, sometimes good player performances go under the radar, as the producers of the match reel are forced to cut out 90% of what actually happened.

This is where statistics come into their own. They paint a full canvas of the weekend's football for those who don't have time to watch every single match. Statistics can also be aggregated. Our memories of events which occurred six Gameweeks ago will inevitably fade, but statistics capture them in their totality and present them clearly and easily for us to reflect on.

I used to practically live inside the Opta Stats Sandbox area on the Fix website. It is a great tool and the one I could least be without, however; I used it a lot for article research and only sparingly for my own FPL decisions. I plan to change that next season.

In addition to this, I will narrow my focus to non-penalty expected goal involvements (Fix has a similar compound metric called Expected FPL Points which translates expected data – including clean sheets – into an FPL specific value). I will also incorporate shot volume into my checks, while disregarding other, less meaningful, metrics.

4. Go back to forward planning

When I talk about 'going back to basics', this is exactly what I mean. I have always been an effective planner. What usually happens is I put together a plan, which soon becomes disrupted by injuries, managerial changes and new information. When this occurs, I adapt accordingly and tweak the plan. This has always worked very well for me.

This last season, I have actually been quite fortunate with injuries and yet – for reasons difficult to fathom – I have not stuck to the plan, when I could/should have. Instead of sticking to the plan, I became distracted by noise and tempted by short-term punts. Yes, there have been times when I have been seriously unfortunate, but I have also put myself in difficult situations with bad decision-making, particularly switching out premium midfielders.

The one thing which bonds the Elite XI group together, despite the broad spectrum of playing styles, is their ability to forward plan effectively. This is something I normally do well, but that I allowed to slip in the 2023/24 season. To improve, I will eliminate short-term punts (unless the strategy allows for it, for example when dead ending into a Wildcard) and focus on a six-Gameweek horizon.

5. Try to make FPL more fun

The most important thing about FPL is that it should be fun. Yes, of course FPL managers will experience ups and downs throughout a season. This is an inevitable part of the journey. But overall, FPL should be enjoyable. The last couple of seasons have not been as much fun for me, which seems somewhat paradoxical, as the schedule has been a lot more stable than it was in the Covid-affected years which preceded them. I can't quite put my finger on what it is, but I intend to invest some serious thought into it over the summer break and implement whatever changes may arise from my conclusion.

An easy excuse would be to blame it on what is shaping up to be my worst ever finish in almost two decades of playing. But it feels like it is deeper than that. The season before I finished around 80k and I felt the same way then. Likewise, I have had poor ranks in the past and never lost my FPL mojo to the same degree.

If I were to 'shoot from the hip' for an explanation, I would say that joining FPL Twitter has played some part in this. When I first joined in late 2020, I was amazed by the online FPL community and viewed it as an absolute gift. But as time has progressed, my attention has shifted away from my mini-leagues and personal rivalries and more to the global competition.

Of all the mini-leagues I am currently a member of, about 50% have more than 100 people in them, most of whom I don't even know personally. I have found that I am not interested in how I am doing in any of these leagues, so why am I even in them? This is certainly something I will explore further.

In the same way I plan to curate my information intake better (as Andrew mentioned earlier), I also need to manage my social media use to make the FPL experience more enjoyable. How this will look, I do not yet know. But certainly, I will move away from posting my teams weekly, will minimise the number of group chats I am in, and will do what is necessary to feel less beholden to a certain playing style. Flexibility is king.

THE FUTURE OF FPL

I certainly hope that you've gained some insight from this book, which will enable you to raise your game going forwards. Being immersed in the Elite XI has been a rewarding experience, but often confusing for me. Often, the myriad of different playing styles was contradictory when trying to take in the opinions of some of the world's greatest FPL players. Laying the information out in this book has helped me turn all that noise into a coherent plan. I now feel like I know what I should keep doing, which bad habits to drop, and what new things I should try next season.

But one of the things the Elite XI group is very proficient at is being able to adapt to changes. In that sense it is worth asking, what about the future of FPL?

FPL RULE CHANGES

Let's start with what we already know. On the very eve of this book's publication, FPL Towers announced a raft of changes which will have a bearing on the 2024/25 season. I haven't had a great deal of time to process these changes, but here I will offer my initial thoughts and how the changes will impact FPL managers.

Five stackable free transfers

This is by far the biggest change FPL has announced, and the impact on strategy could be far-reaching for engaged managers and casuals alike. In simple terms, FPL managers will now be able to accrue five free transfers, where this cap was previously set at two.

In addition, playing your Wildcard or Free Hit chip would once 'burn' any accrued free transfers in the subsequent Gameweek; this is no longer the case. Now, an FPL manager could save up their transfers to the maximum limit, play their Wildcard in a Gameweek, then have five free transfers to make in the very next Gameweek.

This is actually quite a shrewd move from FPL, for the following reasons:

1. It will provide more planning opportunities and transfer divergence for engaged managers.

[171]

2. It will be far better for casuals who will have an opportunity to sort their team out, if – as is common – they have a small period away from the game and find their team to be in a mess.

3. Rolled free transfers not being wiped out by chip deployment broadens Wildcard and Free Hit strategy options, meaning even further tactical divergence.

My gut tells me that this will benefit casual players more, offering them a route out of trouble if they have time off from the game and their squad needs major attention upon their return. I cannot visualise a scenario where even the most long-term focused manager racks up five free transfers. Only in the event of extraordinary planning and good fortune would this happen. In most cases, the short-term damage of not making any transfers would be too great.

A potential impact this may have is widening the gap between those who get off to a good start and those who don't. Should the planets align for an FPL manager early on, then this manager can begin to accrue free transfers while racking up points and already owning the most popular players. Those who don't get off to a good start will be fire-fighting during this same period. Come Gameweek 6, those with good overall ranks will be ahead on both FPL points and accrued free transfers. This means getting a good start could be more important than ever.

There may also be some benefit for aggressive players who can make solid, short-term gains while the more risk averse managers bank their transfers and lose rank in the process. This could, however, come full circle when the long-term planners deploy their banked transfers and make major structural changes to their squads.

Bonus Points System (BPS) and scoring changes

There have also been some changes to the BPS scoring, which could have an impact on our player selection. They are:

Goalkeeper penalty saves

When a goalkeeper saves a penalty, the BPS score will be reduced to 9 (down from 15). This is intended to reduce the 'double whammy' effect whereby a goalkeeper is disproportionately rewarded for a penalty save, having already been awarded 5 FPL points for the same occurrence.

Conceding goals

As well as losing their clean sheet points, goalkeepers and defenders will now lose 4 BPS points for each goal conceded, which will further penalise players of teams who concede more than one goal in a game. This somewhat lessens the potential for generating points from defensive duties alone, although this is somewhat counter balanced by the next change.

Off the line clearances

There are few things as exciting as seeing a defender visibly praised by their relieved teammates after some goal line heroics, in which they save their team from conceding what looks to be an inevitable goal.

This exciting aspect will now be reflected in the BPS scoring, with any player who makes a goal line clearance being rewarded with 3 BPS points. This is, however, such a rare occurrence that it will unlikely make any practical difference to our player selections.

Being fouled and shots on target

Two straightforward changes. If a player is awarded a foul, he gets 1 added to his BPS score. Players who often draw fouls will benefit most from this change.

In addition, any player who registers a shot on target will earn an extra 2 BPS. Of all the changes, this is probably the most significant. The players who top the tables for both being fouled and shots on target – for example Phil Foden in the 2023/24 season – are much more likely to earn bonus points.

Targeting these players could be a good move next season.

What the above actually serves to do is take BPS potential away from defenders and give it to attackers. My feeling is that goalkeepers will be more severely punished under the new system as they will get hit twice. Not only will they lose BPS for every goal conceded, but every time they make a save, the outfield player who took the shot will earn extra BPS, thus negating the benefit to the keeper.

Goalkeeper goals

Finally, FPL will now award 10 (rather than 6) points per goal scored by your goalkeeper. I can't really argue with the logic. However, this is such a rare occurrence that it hardly warrants any excitement.

Mystery chip

A somewhat unusual move, FPL has announced the release of a mystery chip, the details of which are, well, mysterious.

All we know is that we will not be able to use it until January 2025, and that its purpose will be revealed "ahead of January 2025, so that you plan ahead before the chip becomes playable".

What this could be? Who knows?

A calmer schedule?

In April 2024, the Football Association's chief executive, Mark Bullingham, declared that an agreement to scrap FA Cup replays would secure "a strong format for the future". This is in part due to the expansion of European football from next season. Players, managers and teams from the Premier League are likely to welcome this news, as it will potentially remove a fixture which will need to be played using already-stretched squads. Teams lower down in the football pyramid, who stand to lose lots of revenue from the decision, are understandably furious.

Whichever side of the fence you sit on, this will have an impact on the Premier League schedule next season, which, in turn, will have implications for FPL planning. A decent proportion of both blank and double Gameweek fixtures are caused by FA Cup replays which will now no longer occur. This means the future schedule should be calmer and easier to plan for.

This will be music to the ears of the more casual player. However, for engaged managers, the news probably isn't as sweet. Most engaged managers I know enjoy the chaos caused by blank and double Gameweeks. Producing spreadsheets and fixture tables to navigate the chaos is one of the great joys for many managers. It also offers an opportunity for engaged managers to make ground on the 'casuals' by planning ahead with transfers and/or maximising chip effectiveness.

Other managers, particularly those who have been playing for a while, may welcome the news, as they harken back to simpler days when your transfers and captaincy decisions held the key to a good rank, rather than gaining an edge by navigating anomalies in the schedule.

Whichever camp you sit in, this is a real change coming our way and will have a serious impact on chip and transfer strategy, starting with the 2024/25 season.

*

So that covers what we know. But what about potential changes in the seasons beyond?

Advances in AI

The number of people using algorithms to predict player performance is growing exponentially. In a recent survey I carried out on FPL Twitter, over 25% of managers said that they use some form of AI-based modelling to guide their FPL decisions.

As with all areas of life, AI is improving at an alarming rate. Recent advances in artificial intelligence include machines learning through observation, robots acting as caregivers, AI being used to brew beer, and diagnosing medical data such as X-rays. In fact, there is currently AI software which can detect cancerous cells from scans more effectively than the best-trained radiologists. AI used to fly fighter planes can currently beat the best human pilots in simulated dogfights.

But AI is already becoming commonly used in our homes and workplaces thanks to the massive practical benefits of AI assistants on smartphones. The advancement of AI is only going in one direction. And at an exponential rate.

Already, algorithm-based player predictions are helping users gain immense ranks. Fix's Assistant Manager tool, OptiBot, is amongst the first and is one of the best out there, often beating the competition when predicting the best Free Hit team.[31] Imagine how powerful future iterations of these programs will be for predicting player success. When this happens, those who aren't using these tools will be at a major disadvantage.

Other potential changes coming to FPL

On top of the changes we know – or can predict with a high degree of certainty – are coming, there are other changes which could be on the horizon. What

---

[31] A feature which is showcased on the weekly 'Eddie vs The Algorithm' YouTube video.

these could be, we do not yet know, but we will have to adapt accordingly if and when they arise.

If you ask ten different people what they would like to see changed in FPL, you will probably get ten different answers. But here are some examples of desired potential changes, which I see mentioned often:

Gameweek deadline moved to first kick-off – This is probably the change the masses would most like to see. While it is one I personally do not want implemented, I can see the logic in it, especially as it would solve the problem of early team leaks.

As I have said repeatedly, early team leaks are a scourge on the game. They force people to be glued to their computers on a Friday night or Saturday morning, with a list of possible transfer iterations based on the starting line-up of the first game. This offers an advantage over the less engaged, making for an unfair playing field. There is also no guarantee that the information is correct, so an element of risk still needs to be taken into account. Even if the leaked team sheet turns out to be correct, there's no guarantee that you will be able to make your transfers in time, as the FPL servers are prone to crashing when transfer activity reaches a peak. This creates a messy cocktail of pre-deadline stress.

Moving the deadline in line with first kick-off solves some but not all of these issues. The major benefit of this change would be fairness. No longer can the select few, who are privy to private information, benefit over those who don't have access to the leaks. It also ends the problem of unreliable sources. If the team sheets have been announced, then we can make our transfers with confidence, rather than hoping an anonymous source happens to be correct.

The problem of timing would still remain, however. A move to a pre-kick-off deadline would invariably mean that, just as at present, we would be forced to wait until just before first kick-off to make our moves. Not doing so would be negligent, as you would be making transfers when you were not in possession of all the facts. This will be highly inconvenient for those who have plans at this time. For me, personally, I don't want to be glued to the computer on a Friday night when I should be reading with my kids. Nor do I want to be stuck to the chair in my study on a Saturday morning, when I should be out walking the dog or engaging in family time. I realise not everyone shares this view, and many are happy to be attached to their computer at these times. Nevertheless, it will impact how FPL fits into our lives.

Whether FPL will implement this change, who knows? There are a number of other, smaller fantasy football games (such as Sky Sports Fantasy Football) that have their transfer deadline in line with the first kick-off. Implementing this for FPL would require a beefy upgrade to their servers in order to handle the traffic peaks which would occur once the line-ups had been announced.

Transparency around price changes – A close second is transparency around price changes. Fantasy Football Fix uses an incredibly accurate algorithm in their Price Change Predictor tool to warn users of potential rises and falls. But each season this algorithm needs to self-correct, or be manually tweaked by the behind-the-scenes wizards who work on the development team. Even then, there are some price changes which defy all known parameters. This suggests some degree of manual tinkering occurs behind the scenes at FPL Towers.

As I have said previously, I don't prioritise building/retaining team value (for reasons I won't elaborate on here) but it is annoying nevertheless when a transfer target, or soon-to-be-outgoing player, changes price just a couple of days before you plan to transfer them out. Knowing this in advance can help but usually requires consciously taking the price change 'on the chin' or taking a slight risk by going early (and finding out in the press conference that they've picked up a knock on the training ground).

[181]

What is really frustrating is when you take a chance due to an upcoming price change, which then doesn't happen. Or, conversely, you are stung by a price change which wasn't meant to happen.

I don't see why FPL doesn't make their price changes transparent. They could easily design a system which shows when a player's price is about to go up or down, then managers can make an informed decision as to how to proceed. This would make managing your budget much more straightforward. Until then, Fix's Price Change Predictor is the best way of staying apprised of any changes.

HOW SHOULD WE DEFINE ELITE?

As the focus of this book has been an exercise in 'becoming an elite FPL manager', it is well worth taking a moment to define what 'elite' is.

The *Oxford English Dictionary*'s definition of the word is:

A select group that is superior in terms of ability or qualities to the rest of a group or society.

The problem is, there is no agreed and established definition of what constitutes elite in terms of someone's FPL history. How many seasons must you have under your belt to achieve elite status? If somebody has played for two seasons and racked 2 x Top 1k finishes, does that make them elite, or must they prove themselves over a longer period? If so, how long?

If someone has 6 x Top 10k finishes, but has finished outside the Top 1m on two occasions, does this make them elite? Or do the bad finishes tarnish an otherwise 'elite' FPL career?

Then, of course, we have to factor luck into it. If you accept the premise that FPL is 50% luck and 50% skill, you must also accept that the FPL elite, however you recognise them, are in this hallowed group as much from their good fortune as their skill at FPL.

The point is, what people consider 'elite' is inevitably subjective. I imagine most people would want to see at least two (and probably more) Top 10k finishes in someone's career history before they even considered having a conversation about them being elite. Also, the bottom end can be important too. If someone has two or more Top 10k finishes, but four or five finishes in the Top 250k, then I think the bad finishes will start to erode people's desire to consider them as elite.

When I wrote my book *FPL Obsessed: Tips for Success in Fantasy Premier League*, I felt that a Top 100k finish was one that anyone should be proud of, but a season inside the Top 10k was an elite finish. This seems to be a fairly common barometer for FPL success.

But has the time come for us to re-assess these milestones?

There's a great Fix tool called FPL Statistics; this tool has a feature which allows the user to remove what it deems 'inactive squads' from the statistics presented. Inactive squads are defined as those in which no change has been made in the last five Gameweeks, a pretty robust indication that the user is not playing FPL seriously. I always keep my eye on this. At around the halfway point of the season, roughly 40% of registered teams are inactive. As the season progresses, this usually creeps past 50%.

If, for the sake of argument, we say that you are competing – in real terms – with 50% of registered teams, then this would be around 5.4m engaged players who play every week and until the end of the season. It then gets complicated, because an unknown number of these teams will be 'experimental' or 'second' teams from already registered users. This is, of course, against FPL rules, but as long as these managers keep their heads down and alter their team details, the chances are FPL will never find out about them.

Nevertheless, the number of inactive squads has probably always been roughly proportional to the total number of registered players, and hence your final overall rank should be viewed as a proportion of the total registered squads that year. To give an example, my best finish was 2,489 in 2010/11. In that year, there were only 2.4m registered squads. This means I was roughly in the Top 0.1% of players that year. Impressive, but that same rank this year would have meant I was in the Top 0.02% of players.

Let's put this another way. A coveted Top 10k in the 2006/07 season would mean you were in the Top 0.5% of players. This is roughly equivalent to a Top 100k finish in the 2022/23 season (0.8%). Perhaps it's time to say that an elite finish in the modern era is bagging a Top 50k. And anywhere inside the Top 200k is a respectable season.

How we define success has an impact on the decisions we make to achieve the goals we set ourselves. Many FPL managers are becoming frustrated by how difficult the game has become. Not only are we all competing against more players, but we are competing against better and more informed players.

In past seasons, the best and worst players were separated by skill, research and dedication. This is no longer the case. Casuals can now keep pace with highly engaged managers, thanks to the explosion of refined and accessible information which is available everywhere. AI, podcasts, YouTube channels, dedicated websites. If you don't enjoy FPL research, but still want to win your work mini-league, why not copy the moves of a YouTuber or Elite XI manager who bags a decent finish every season? The prize pot is likely to pay for your subscription fees, with money left over.

This is the world of FPL we now live in. Getting a top finish has never been more challenging but, hopefully, using the tips you have learned in this book, you can put yourself in the best possible position to become an elite FPL manager.

ACKNOWLEDGEMENTS

I would first like to thank Tom Brown, who is the glue that holds together all the elements of Fix. I'm yet to meet anyone who is not regularly in the public eye who is so intensely on the pulse of what is happening in the FPL world. He is one of the nicest guys you will ever meet, with a cracking sense of humour, and he taught me a lot about working in the online world. Without him giving me the opportunity to work with Fix and become so immersed in the Elite XI concept, this book wouldn't have been possible.

Thanks also go to Sam and Adam for creating a fantastic company which conducts itself with integrity and passion. Like this book, and its predecessor, Fantasy Football Fix was created out of a love for FPL. It has been run, and still is run, to put the user experience before profit.

Finally, I would like to thank all the Elite XI managers with whom I have spent the last two years discussing FPL at both a specific and a philosophical level. The passion and research they all put into the management of their FPL teams is breathtaking. It is also astounding (and encouraging) that people with such different playing styles can so repeatedly attain elite finishes. It is an honour to be exposed to such a level of talent and allow privileged knowledge to be passed on 'by osmosis' into this book.

In particular, I would like to thank Mark Mansfield, James Cooper and Andrew Neave. Their contributions to this book have been invaluable; and Mark, I promise I will listen to your warnings about 'chasing doublers instead of points' in the future.

But a very special thanks must go out to Corey Baker and Craig Reumert. As well as each contributing to this book by way of a special case study, these two chaps have saved my bacon on many occasions in the years I have spent with Fix. Craig is one of the most genuinely funny people I have ever met, and Corey is possibly the most intensely sports-obsessed person on the planet. Both of them were always willing – at seemingly any point – to drop everything to help me out with an FPL deadline if I needed to throw together an article. For that you have my sincerest thanks.

I'd also like to show my immense gratitude to those who bought my previous book, especially those who were kind enough to leave a review. The importance of feedback for writers is almost impossible to overstate. If the feedback from this book is even half as good as before, I will consider it a success.

Finally, as always, a huge shout out to every FPL manager out there. It's a crazy old game which often feels more like a slog and a commitment than a bit of fun, yet we do it every season for better or worse. Without you, it wouldn't be anywhere near as good.

APPENDIX A – LUCK IN FPL SURVEY

13 respondents

1. How big a role does luck play in consistent FPL success (the balance being skill, discipline etc.)?

   Less than 30% = 5 (38%)
   30% – 40% = 5 (38%)
   40% – 50% = 0 (0%)
   Exactly 50% = 1 (8%)
   50% – 60% = 1 (8%)
   60% – 70% = 0 (0%)
   More than 70% = 1 (8%)

2. Do you consider yourself to be lucky (as well as being skilful) to have earned such a good FPL history?

   Yes (both luck and skill) = 9 (69%)
   No (just skilful) = 4 (31%)
   No (just lucky) = 0 (0%)

3. Do you consider yourself to be good at recognising the difference between good/bad FPL choices and good/bad luck?

   Yes = 13 (100%)
   No = 0 (0%)

4. Do you know any FPL managers who you would consider to be highly skilled but are frequently unlucky?

Yes, one or two = 4 (31%)
Yes, quite a few = 2 (15%)
Yes, plenty = 0 (0%)
No, none at all = 7 (54%)

5. Do you know any FPL managers who you would consider to be unskilled, but are frequently lucky?

Yes, one or two = 3 (23%)
Yes, quite a few = 4 (31%)
Yes, plenty = 0 (0%)
No, none at all = 6 (46%)

Comments

- Luck plays a big role in the short term, but consistent success is down to skill for the vast majority.
- Luck increases as you rise in rank.
- In the short run luck has a huge impact on the outcome but consistent FPL success is down to skill.
- In one season of course it can have a big bearing, but in terms of 'consistent' (i.e. across seasons) it is less relevant as we are all subject to it.
- Generally, making consistently sensible decisions will bring decent points and ranks. But you still need a good amount of luck. Skill is what you use before every deadline, to put yourself into the best possible position. After that, you're at the mercy of external events you don't have

control over, so maybe it's not 50/50 but you need to get lucky.
- Captains and extra chips make variance greater.

APPENDIX B – ELITE XI COMMON TRAITS

12 respondents

1. What level of importance do you place on self-analysis (looking back at your FPL decisions and objectively evaluating them)?

   Not very important = 3 (25%)
   Somewhat important = 6 (50%)
   Very important = 3 (25%)

2. When a season is over, do you go back and review the season as a whole to identify where you did well, and where you did poorly?

   No, never = 5 (41.67%)
   Sometimes = 2 (16.67%)
   Yes, every season = 5 (41.67%)

3. Do you have a social media account dedicated to FPL?

   Yes = 9 (75%)
   No = 3 (25%)

4. Do you consider yourself to be an active and contributing member of the online FPL community?

   Yes, I post about FPL online often = 2 (16.67%)
   I sometimes post about FPL online = 4 (33.33%)
   I have a social media account but I only listen to others, I don't post about FPL = 4 (33.33%)

I don't use social media for FPL at all = 2
(16.67%)

5. Do you believe building team value is important?

Yes, it is important throughout the season = 3
(25%)
Yes, but only at the beginning of the season = 3
(25%)
No, it is not important = 6 (50%)

6. What sources of information do you use to
inform your FPL decisions? (Tick all that apply)

Podcasts = 8 (66.67%)
FPL websites = 9 (75%)
Statistics = 10 (83.33%)
AI prediction tools = 7 (58.33%)
Press conferences = 11 (91.67%)
Trusted sources of team news leaks (ITKs) = 11
(91.67%)
Fans/fan forums of specific teams = 4 (33.33%)
Watching matches live = 10 (83.33%)
Watching highlights (*MOTD* or equivalent) = 10
(83.33%)
Live text = 4 (33.33%)
Discussing with friends/colleagues = 7 (58.33%)
None of the above = 0 (0%)

7. If you have brought in an FPL player and
instantly realised it has been a mistake, would
you be happy to correct your mistake
immediately by transferring that player out
again?

[194]

Yes = 8 (66.67%)
No, because I would always want to give that
player time = 1 (8.33%)
No, because that would be a waste of a transfer
= 3 (25%)

8. Do you consider yourself to be open to objective
feedback, even if that feedback is negative?

Yes, I welcome all feedback = 12 (100%)
I don't like it, but I will listen = 0 (0%)
No, I am not open to feedback = 0 (0%)

APPENDIX C – ELITE XI PLAYING STYLES

9 respondents

1. If you had to choose one, would you choose form or fixtures?

   Form = 0 (0%)
   Fixtures = 9 (100%)

2. Does Effective Ownership play a role in your decision-making

   Yes, a large role = 0 (0%)
   Sometimes = 8 (88.89%)
   No role at all = 1 (11.11%)

3. How a big a role do statistics play in your FPL decisions

   A large role = 5 (55.56%)
   They are quite important = 2 (22.22%)
   Not very important = 2 (22.22%)
   I don't look at stats = 0 (0%)

4. Which stats are most important to you? (Tick the three most important)

   xG = 6 (66.67%)
   NPxG = 7 (77.78%)
   xA = 6 (66.67%)
   Shots = 3 (33.33%)
   Shots on target = 1 (11.11%)
   Shots in the box = 2 (22.22%)
   Big chances = 1 (11.11%)

Big chances created = 1 (11.11%)
Final 1/3 passes = 1 (11.11%)
Crosses = 1 (11.11%)

5. When planning a transfer, how many fixtures ahead do you tend to look (assuming no anomalies such as planned chips, DGWs etc.)?

1–2 Gameweeks = 0 (0%)
3–4 Gameweeks = 2 (22.22%)
5–6 Gameweeks = 7 (77.78%)
7–8 Gameweeks = 0 (0%)
9+ Gameweeks = 0 (0%)

6. When reviewing player/team data to inform your decisions, what historical period of data do you focus most on? (assume you are in the middle of a season)

The last couple of Gameweeks only = 0 (0%)
3–5 Gameweeks = 0 (0%)
6–8 Gameweeks = 5 (55.56%)
9–10 Gameweeks = 1 (11.11%)
The entire season's data = 3 (33.33%)
The entire season plus previous seasons = 0 (0%)

APPENDIX D – ELITE CHIP STRATEGY

10 respondents

1. Would you describe yourself as having a consistent chip strategy?

   No, it is totally different each year = 2 (20%)
   Yes, I stick to the same strategy each season = 2 (20%)
   It is generally the same, but I sometimes deviate = 6 (60%)

2. When do you tend to play your first Wildcard (WC1)?

   In the first four Gameweeks = 0 (0%)
   Gameweeks 5–7 = 5 (50%)
   Gameweeks 8–10 = 2 (20%)
   As late as possible (without losing it) = 3 (30%)

3. When do you tend to play your second Wildcard (WC2)?

   Early on in the new year = 0 (0%)
   Around the middle = 1 (10%)
   Towards the end of the season = 2 (20%)
   Just before a big Double Gameweek = 7 (70%)

4. Would you ever use your Triple Captain in a single Gameweek?

   Yes, and I have done so = 2 (20%)
   Yes, but I haven't yet done it = 0 (0%)
   No, double Gameweeks only = 8 (80%)

5. Would you ever use your Bench Boost chip in a single Gameweek?

   Yes, and I have done so = 3 (30%)
   Yes, but I haven't yet done it = 5 (50%)
   No, double Gameweeks only = 2 (20%)

6. Which of these options best describes your preferred usage of the Free Hit chip?

   To survive a blank Gameweek = 3 (30%)
   To capitalise on a double Gameweek = 6 (60%)
   To navigate a tricky single Gameweek = 1 (10%)
   To navigate a short-term injury crisis = 0 (0%)

7. Which of the non-Wildcard chips is the most powerful?

   Free Hit = 9 (90%)
   Triple Captain = 0 (0%)
   Bench Boost = 1 (10%)

GLOSSARY OF TERMS

Attacking Returns – Usually used in reference to a Defender, attacking returns are points generated from a goal or an assist.

Auto-Substitute – If one of your players plays 0 minutes in a Gameweek, the player on your bench, who is numerically first, will be automatically swapped into your starting XI, as long as this does not lead to an invalid formation.

Bandwagon – Occurs when lots of managers transfer in a player, usually one who was not previously highly owned.

Bench Boost (BB) – One of the four special chips which a manager can play in a Gameweek of their choosing. The Bench Boost allows the points scored by all four bench players to count towards the Gameweek total.

Blank – When a player scores two points or less in a single game. Many consider 3 points to be a blank.

Blank Gameweek (BGW) – Any Gameweek in which there are fewer than ten scheduled fixtures. Players from the teams who are not playing will get 0 points.

Bonus Points System (BPS) – BPS is used to track and reward the players' involvement in the game. Players will accumulate BPS points during the game and, at the end of every game, Bonus Points are given out. Typically, the three best-performing players from each match will receive BPs (3, 2, 1).

Bus Team – When you arrange your team to be the best it can possibly be, prior to making any transfers. Essentially, the squad you would want to go into the next Gameweek, should you be hit by a bus and be unable to change it.

Captain (C) – The player who you select as your captain will get double the points in that Gameweek.

Chips – Chips can be used to (potentially) enhance your team's performance during the season. Only one chip can be used in a single Gameweek.

Clean Sheet (CS) – A clean sheet is awarded to a goalkeeper, defender or midfielder when the team they play for does not concede a goal, so long as they played for at least 60 minutes. Any players substituted after 60 minutes will still receive a Clean Sheet, even if their team goes on to concede a goal.

Dead ending – When a manager makes their transfer decisions with only a select number of Gameweeks in mind, due to the fact that a chip will be played in a specific Gameweek.

Differential – A differential is a low-owned player, be that in overall FPL terms or in the context of a mini-league. There is no universal definition of what constitutes a differential; however, it is widely considered than any player with less than 10% ownership is a differential.

Double-Digit Haul – When a player accrues ten or more points in a single game.

Double Gameweek (DGW) – Any Gameweek in which there are over ten scheduled fixtures. Players from the teams who are playing twice will have their points from both matches combined.

Doubler – A term to describe a player who is playing twice in Gameweek.

Doubling Up – When you have two players from the same team in your squad.

Draft – Draft is a different way to play FPL, where each player can only be owned once in the league.

Effective Ownership (EO) - Percentage of managers who started a player + percentage of managers who captained that player + percentage of managers who triple captained that player – percentage of managers who benched that player.

Enabler(s) – The cheapest available players (£4m goalkeeper and defender, £4.5m midfielder and forward), who enable you to afford higher-value players elsewhere. These players usually sit on the bench.

Essential / Must Have – A player who, in someone's opinion, is crucial to success either in a single Gameweek or over the course of a season.

Expected Assists (xA) – A metric used to identify the likelihood a given pass will become a goal assist.

Expected Goal Involvement (xGI) – A metric used to track players' expected contributions to both goals and assists.

Expected Goals (xG) – A metric used to identify the likelihood a shot will result in a goal.

Fear of missing out (FOMO) – The feeling of pressure FPL managers feel when a player they don't own is being widely praised or discussed. This often leads to the desire to go against a pre-established strategy.

FPL Assist – When FPL award an assist, even if the assist is not being officially awarded in the match.

FPL Cup – The FPL Cup starts midway through the season. Approximately half of the existing managers are automatically eliminated (if their rank is in the bottom half overall), and the remaining managers are pitted against each other in a knockout format; the winner advances to the next round. This happens all the way until GW38, where the last two managers will contest the final.

Free Hit (FH) – One of the four special chips which a manager can play in a Gameweek of their choosing. The Free Hit allows the manager to make unlimited free transfers to their squad for that Gameweek. Unlike the Wildcard (WC), the team will revert back to how it was in the Gameweek prior to the chip being played.

Free Transfers (FTs) – Transfer(s) which a manager can make ahead of the next Gameweek which will not incur a points reduction.

Gameweek (GW) – Defined as the period of time 90 minutes prior to the kick-off of the first match and up until the beginning of the next Gameweek.

Haul – When a player makes more than one return in a single game.

Head-To-Head (H2H) – The two different ways of scoring in the game, either the classic scoring, where points are accumulated, or the H2H scoring, where each week a manager is paired with an opponent in the league. The winner takes three points, draw is one point a piece and zero points for a loss.

Hits (Points Hits) – When a transfer is made, once the Free Transfer has been used. This transfer will come with a four-point deduction from the next

Gameweek score. Points hits are therefore in multiples of four (–4, –8, –12 and so on).

In The Bank (ITB) – The amount of money which is surplus to the budget invested in the 15-man squad.

In The Know (ITK) – People who have connections with the Premier League clubs and are therefore privy to confidential information (such as starting XIs and injury news).

Kneejerk – Reacting to a situation quickly and without due consideration.

Mini-Leagues (MLs) – Leagues which you set up with your friends.

Nailed (On) – A player who is expected to start a match as long as they are not injured.

Non-Penalty Expected Goals (NPxG) – Expected Goals (xG) excluding those from penalties.

Out Of Position (OOP) – Usually in reference to a player whose position has been incorrectly categorised within FPL. Example: John Lundstram was categorised as a Defender in FPL but was playing in midfield for Sheffield United in the 2019/20 season.

Overall Points (OP) – The total sum of points your team has accumulated at any point in the season.

Overall Rank (OR) – The rank/position of your team within FPL's Overall Public League at any given time. This is the league which every registered team is automatically included in.

Over-performing – When a player's actual goal involvement is higher than their xGI.

Points Per Game (PPG) – The average number of points a player returns in a Gameweek (Total Points / Number of Games Played).

Points Per Game Per Million (PPG/M) – A ratio of Points Per Game against the cost of the player (used to ascertain a player's value).

Premium/Heavy Hitter – A player who is in the upper price bracket of any given position. There is no approved definition of what the price brackets are but, generally: a Defender is valued at £6m+ and a Midfielder/Forward is £10m+.

Pressers – Premier League press conferences.

Punt – Usually used in reference to a risky or differential transfer.

Rage Transfer – When a transfer is made by somebody who is still angry about something which has taken place in the Gameweek.

Red Card (RC) – When a player is sent off (three points are deducted).

Return – When a player earns any number of points in a single game, besides the two points obtained for playing over 60 minutes. Many consider four points to be necessary to constitute a return.

Squad Value (SV) – The value of your 15-man squad net of money In The Bank (ITB).

Starting XI – The eleven players which form your squad who are not on the bench. Only your starting XI can generate points (unless a Bench Boost has been played).

Template – A hypothetical team comprising the most highly owned players.

Triple Captain (TC) – One of the four chips which a manager can play in a Gameweek of their choosing. The Triple Captain multiplies the selected captain's Gameweek points by three instead of two.

Tripling Up – When you have three players (the maximum permitted) from the same team in your squad.

Underlying Stats – An umbrella term for any statistics which evaluate a player's performance but are not as obvious as Goals, Assists, Clean Sheets, Points, etc.

Under-performing – When a player's actual goal involvement is lower than their xGI.

Vice-Captain (VC) – The player selected to become your Captain (C) in the event that your Captain plays 0 minutes in that Gameweek.

Wildcard (WC) – One of the four chips which a manager can play in a Gameweek of their choosing. When the Wildcard is activated, managers can make unlimited free transfers in that Gameweek only.

Wildcard 1 (WC1) – WC1 can be played in the first half of the season. It will be lost if it is not played prior to the designated Gameweek.

Wildcard 2 (WC2) – WC2 can be played in the second half of the season. It will be lost if it is not played prior to GW38.

Yellow Card (YC) – When a player is booked (1 point is deducted).

FIX TOOLS

The following is a non-exhaustive list of FPL tools available on the Fix website. There are too many to list here, so I shall focus on the ones which I use the most.

Fixture Ticker – This tool allows users to check the upcoming fixture difficulty of every Premier League team. You can check the period of Gameweeks to focus on and omit any Gameweeks from the schedule. It is also split into defensive and attack difficulty rather than aggregated like FPL's official one. Difficulty ratings are dynamic, so when a team improves/declines during a season, this is reflected in real time. Finally, the colour coding has multiple shades, allowing a more nuanced view than the standard four colours offered by the official FPL FDR.

Opta Stats Sandbox – Using Opta's own data, this is the go to area for all stats. The user interface is well laid out and the stats grids are tabulated by type. The default tab is Key Stats (the most commonly used) such as xG, xA, and xFPL (Fix's own metric discussed earlier). There are tons of filters and toggle to switch between player and team stats.

Price Change Predictor – I check this all week to see if any of my in/out transfer targets are about to change in price. An essential tool for anyone building or preserving team value.

Future Planner – This tool is an absolute game changer for planners. This area shows your current squad but allows you to make moves Gameweeks into the future. This is essential for budget management and gives you a feel of how transfer plans are going to look down the line. It links to the other tools (such as Fixture Planner and Player Points Projections) to aid in the decision-making process.

Insight Live – This tool offers a plethora of data relating to live Gameweek statistics. It is here that users can find current ownership stats at various rank tiers, as well as average points, captaincy, transfer data, etc. A useful place when making big strategic decisions.

Elite XI: Team Reveal – This is the hub, described earlier, where Premium users can access real-time data from the Elite XI managers. The Consensus XI shows the aggregated and current most owned squad amongst the elite managers. Users can use push or email notifications to keep up to date with the managers' moves. The Manager Mindset section offers a running commentary of why the Elite XI are making their selections.

Player Points Projections – An AI-powered tool which predicts the number of points a player is going to score in a given Gameweek. These predictions are updated constantly, and in real time, as new information becomes available.

Opta Player Heatmaps – For those who like statistics represented graphically, this tool uses the wealth of Opta data available to show player heatmaps, shot location and type, player average positions. It also uses radar graphics for player comparisons. Full of filters and data tabs, this is a really versatile tool.

Fix Comparison Matrix – If your transfer decision has come down to a number of candidates, this is a great place to put them side by side for a direct comparison. Visually stunning to look at, this area can be arranged by custom statistics, meaning the players can be compared using the stats which are most important to you.

Assistant Manager – The AI hub of Fantasy Football Fix, the assistant manager tool offers impartial advice free from emotion and bias. This area is based around your current squad. It is here OptiBot can make transfer suggestions and give squad optimisation advice such as optimal captaincy and bench decisions.

Gameweek Live – A great place to watch the live action unfold. With a live Opta Match Events feed, users can see events in real time and see the impact they are having on your squad (beware, this is not always a positive thing!)

FPL Statistics – A useful tool when reflecting on what has happened so far. This area has statistics on ownership, points scored, captaincy, player and team value, most commonly used formations, and chip statistics.

LEAVING A REVIEW

If you enjoyed this book, then please leave a customer review on either Amazon or Goodreads.

As an author, customer reviews are a vital source of feedback from my readers. They also help others, who are considering reading the book, to have the confidence to make the purchase. Sadly, less than 10% of readers actually go on to leave a review on a book.

If you have five minutes to spare, please give me your genuine thoughts on the book. If you are pushed for time, feel free to drop a one-liner letting me know what you think.

Your reviews will be greatly appreciated.

If you have any feedback you would like to give direct to me, you can contact me on:

Twitter: twitter.com/fpl_obsessed

ABOUT THE AUTHOR

Matt Whelan lives in Chester, North West England and is the author of *FPL Obsessed: Tips for Success at Fantasy Premier League* and the children's interactive fantasy series *Adventure Quest*. He is a freelance copyeditor, SEO copywriter, and writes articles for a number of websites.

While his father nurtured his love of the fantasy and science fiction genres, it was Matt's uncle, Steve, who introduced him to Liverpool Football Club and a lifelong love of football.

In 2004, Matt was introduced to Fantasy Premier League (FPL) which broadened his enjoyment of footy beyond Liverpool's matches. He has been an FPL enthusiast ever since.

When not making his transfers, he can be found spending time with his wife and two children or throwing a ball for his dog Alfie.

Printed in Great Britain
by Amazon

54175180R00126